MW00855920

GETTYSBURG

ALSO BY BRUCE CHADWICK

The Cannons Roar

GETTYSBURG

THE TIDE TURNS

BRUCE CHADWICK

PEGASUS BOOKS
NEW YORK LONDON

GETTYSBURG

Pegasus Books, Ltd.
148 West 37th Street, 13th Floor
New York, NY 10018

First Pegasus Books cloth edition February 2025

Interior design by Maria Fernandez

Library of Congress Cataloging-in-Publication Data is available.

ISBN: 978-1-63936-825-9

10 9 8 7 6 5 4 3 2 1

Printed in the United States of America

Distributed by Simon & Schuster
www.pegasusbooks.com

For Joan

Contents

People in the Story, North and South

South

Confederate Army:

J. B. Clifton
James Hodam
Leonidas Torrence
William Seymour
Heros von Borcke
Private W. C. Ward
Corporal Napier Bartlett
Lieutenant G. W. Beale
Lieutenant J. F. J. Caldwell
Lieutenant Frank Dawson
Lieutenant John Dooley
Lieutenant George Finley
Lieutenant Thomas Goree
Lieutenant Randolph McKim
Lieutenant William Pettit
Captain Edward Baird
Captain William Goldsborough
Captain Decimus et Ultimus Barziza
Captain John Holmes Smith
Major John Daniel
Major William Poague
Lieutenant Colonel W. W. Blackford
Lieutenant Colonel Samuel Johnston
Lieutenant Colonel Moxley Sorrel
Colonel E. Porter Alexander
Colonel Archibald Godwin
Colonel William Lowrance

Colonel John Mosby
Colonel William C. Oates
Colonel William Youngblood
General George Anderson
General James Archer
General Lewis Armistead
General William Barksdale
General John Chambliss
General Patrick Cleburne
General Junius Daniel
General Jubal Early
General Richard Ewell
General Richard Garnett
General John Gordon
General Wade Hampton
General Henry Heth
General Ambrose P. Hill
General John Bell Hood
General John Imboden
General Joseph Johnston
General James Kemper
General Robert E. Lee
General Armistead Long
General James Longstreet
General Lafayette McLaws
General James Pettigrew
General George Pickett
General Roger Atkinson Pryor
General Stephen Ramseur
General Robert Rodes
General Paul Semmes
General J. E. B. Stuart
General Richard Taylor

General Isaac Trimble
General Cadmus Wilcox
General Ambrose Wright

Government:
President Jefferson Davis
Chief Commissary Officer Ralph Moses

Civilians:
Mary Chesnut, Southern diarist
Harry Handerson, born in the North, moved to Louisiana
Helen Longstreet, wife of General James Longstreet
Charles Pickett, brother of General George Pickett
Sallie Pickett, wife of General George Pickett

North
Union Army:
Amos Hostetter
Henry Matrau
Leigh Webber
Private Augustus Buell
Private Robert Carter
Private Theodore Gerrish
Corporal Thomas Galway
Lieutenant L. L. Crounse
Lieutenant Alonzo Cushing
Lieutenant John Garden
Lieutenant Charles Hazlett
Lieutenant Frank Haskell
Lieutenant Marcellus Jones
Lieutenant Washington Roebling
Lieutenant Abner Small
Lieutenant Malbone Watson

Lieutenant Jesse Bowman Young
Captain Charles Francis Adams
Captain John Bigelow
Captain Henry C. Coates
Captain Bernhard Domschcke
Captain Samuel Fiske
Captain Amos Hostetter
Captain William Paine
Captain Winfield Scott
Captain James Smith
Captain Benjamin Thompson
Major James Biddle
Major Rufus Dawes
Major St. Clair Mulholland
Major Edmund Rice
Major General D. H. Rucker
Major H. E. Tremain
Major Charles Wainwright
Lieutenant Colonel Freeman McGilvery
Lieutenant Colonel Thomas Hyde
Lieutenant Colonel Theodore Lyman
Lieutenant Colonel William Brooke Rawle
Colonel Joshua Chamberlain
Colonel William Colvill
Colonel Richard Coulter
Colonel Abner Doubleday
Colonel Lucius Fairchild
Colonel George Greene
Colonel Patrick Guiney
Colonel Huntington Jackson
Colonel Patrick O'Rorke
Colonel William Tilton
Colonel Charles Town

Colonel Strong Vincent
General Francis Barlow
General James Barnes
General David Birney
General John Buford
General Daniel Butterfield
General George McClellan
General George Armstrong Custer
General Elon Farnsworth
General John Geary
General John Gibbon
General Ulysses S. Grant
General David McMurtrie Gregg
General Henry Halleck
General Winfield Scott Hancock
General Herman Haupt
General Alexander Hays
General Joseph Hooker
General Oliver Otis Howard
General Andrew Humphreys
General Henry Hunt
General Hugh Judson Kilpatrick
General George Meade
General John Newton
General Marsena Patrick
General Alfred Pleasonton
General John Reynolds
General Carl Schurz
General Winfield Scott
General John Sedgwick
General Daniel Sickles
General Henry Slocum
General George Sykes

General Régis de Trobriand
General Gouverneur Warren
General Alexander Webb
General Stephen Weed
General Alpheus Williams
General Samuel Zook

Government:
Governor Andrew Curtin of Pennsylvania
Assistant Secretary of War Charles Dana
John Hay, Lincoln's private secretary
President Abraham Lincoln
President James Madison
John George Nicolay, Lincoln's private secretary
Frederick Law Olmsted, US Sanitary Commission
Assistant Secretary of War Colonel Thomas A. Scott
Secretary of State William Seward
General George Sharpe, head of the Bureau of Military Information
Senator Charles Sumner of Massachusetts
Secretary of War Edwin Stanton
Secretary of the Navy Gideon Welles

Civilians
Nellie Aughinbaugh, Gettysburg resident
Edward Everett, statesman and orator
Amelia Harmon, Gettysburg resident
Sarah Jane Hoffman, Gettysburg resident
Liberty Hollinger, Gettysburg resident
Henry Eyster Jacobs, student at Gettysburg College
Michael Jacobs, professor of mathematics and chemistry, Pennsylvania College
Ward Lamon, Lincoln's bodyguard and personal friend

William McDougall, Canadian diplomat
Tillie Pierce, Gettysburg resident
John Rummel, Gettysburg farmer
S. C. Shriver, Union Mills resident
J. Howard Wert, Gettysburg resident
Susan White, Gettysburg resident
David Wills, Gettysburg attorney

Neutral:
Spencer Cavendish, the Marquis of Hartington, British observer
Mary Raymond Shipman Andrews, novelist
William Faulkner, novelist

Journalists:
Bonaparte, *New York World*
Charles Coffin, *Boston Journal*
Arthur Fremantle, British journalist
Joseph Gilbert, Associated Press
Horace Greeley, *New-York Tribune*
E. A. Paul, *New York Times*
Samuel Wilkeson, *New York Times*

Historians:
William Blackstone
Edwin Coddington
Shelby Foote
Douglas Southall Freeman
William Herndon, Lincoln's law partner and biographer
Robert Krick
James McPherson
William Garrett Piston
Glenn Tucker

Introduction

July 1, 1863

Gettysburg, Pennsylvania, was a thriving small town in early July 1863. It was home to 2,400 residents and contained 450 buildings, wooden and brick, that housed various small shops and several industries, such as carriage manufacturers, shoemakers, and tanneries There was a bank and one tavern. Ten roads led into and out of Gettysburg, which was not far from the state capital of Harrisburg. A train link ran from Harrisburg to Gettysburg, but it had been shut down. It was a peaceful place; there were several signs in the village that warned residents they would be fined for discharging firearms.

Everyone in America knows the name of that small village today. But Gettysburg should never have been the site of the most famous and consequential battle of the Civil War—one that turned the tide of the conflict in the North's favor and resulted in the bloodiest fight in American history, with more than 50,000 casualties, or about one-third of the total number of troops engaged on both sides of the three-day confrontation. It was General Robert E. Lee's second invasion of the North. It would be his last.

This oral history, *Gettysburg: The Tide Turns*, starts by explaining how both armies accidentally collided on that July 1, 1863. The Northern Army of the Potomac had lost its commander, General Joseph Hooker, who had resigned (to President Abraham Lincoln's delight). General George Meade had replaced him just seventy-two hours before the armies confronted each other at Gettysburg. The Confederate Army of Northern Virginia, led by the legendary and "invincible," it appeared, General Robert E. Lee, had crossed into the North and was trying to find and destroy Meade's army. Lee believed that if he could do that, he could advance on Harrisburg, seize a railroad, take his army into Philadelphia, and capture it in just a few hours. That might have forced President Abraham Lincoln to sue for peace and ended the war.

Meade was trying to do the same thing. He was under great pressure from Lincoln to destroy Lee's mercurial Army of Northern Virginia, fresh off its surprising and stunning victories over Union forces at Fredericksburg and Chancellorsville two months earlier. At Chancellorsville, in Virginia, Lee defeated the army led by General "Fighting Joe" Hooker (whom he assumed he would meet again in southern Pennsylvania) and prevailed against forces twice as large as his own. On top of that, he won the battle by splitting his army in two, something rarely done. Lee was immediately seen as "the wizard." In that battle he lost his second in command, General "Stonewall" Jackson, who was accidentally killed by his own men.

As they crossed into Pennsylvania, neither Meade nor Lee knew where the other was and the size of their forces. (The Union forces numbered more than 100,000 men and the Southerners about 72,000.)

They found each other on the morning of July 1, beginning a horrific three-day battle that would, in the end, determine whether the United States would remain one country or two. It is a story that has been told time and time again in books, movies, lectures, and documentaries, but never—and I do not understand why—as an oral history.

The beauty of the oral history, no matter what the subject, is that, using many sources, a historian brings in the people who were part of the story, large and small in importance, to tell it. All the books about Gettysburg (and there are dozens) are standard stories. The historian tells a tale that is peppered with quotes and narrative, and they choreograph the eyewitness testimony to develop the dramatic overall story. In an oral history, the people in the tale tell it. This type of story gives the reader a chance to consider what many people have to say and adds nuance and personal analysis to the tale. I did that with my previous book about Fort Sumter, and plan to do so again in this work about Gettysburg.

Why was the Battle of Gettysburg so important?

First, it marked the end of Lee's reputation as an unbeatable, mythical general and changed the North's view of him and his army. Second, it ended the South's ideas of invading the North (the battle was called "the high-water mark of the Confederacy"). Third, although Gettysburg, and another Union victory at Vicksburg on the same day as the one at Gettysburg, did not end the war, it began a final chapter that, nearly two years later, did result in that conclusion. Fourth, the defeat at Gettysburg unfurled the "lost cause" banner that the South wrapped itself in and, in the end, made their loss in the Civil War more explainable and understandable to Southerners (moral victory against insurmountable odds). Fifth, it provided several memorable events that have echoed through history, such as the successful Union defense at Little Round Top, led by Maine's Colonel Joshua Chamberlain, and the much-written-about, ill-fated third day attack of the Confederates—Pickett's Charge.

And sixth, Gettysburg gave President Abraham Lincoln the opportunity to deliver his memorable Gettysburg Address, which helped to "bind up the wounds" of the nation—both sides of it—and has lived forever as one of the great speeches in US history.

There were several reasons for the invasion of Pennsylvania. Lee's army was always out of food. His men had drained Virginia of just about all its food; an invasion of Pennsylvania, with its thousands of farms, would bring them all the food and other supplies they so desperately needed. Right up until the middle of June 1863, the Army of the Potomac, under the command of Major General Joseph Hooker, had been lurking around Virginia, dangerously close to Richmond. Then it suddenly turned away from Richmond and marched north. Lee now did not have to worry about protecting Richmond and could march into Pennsylvania.

He also needed horses, and in Pennsylvania he could appropriate as many as he needed from farms there. Thanks to the Northerners abandoning their Virginia campaign, Confederate President Jefferson Davis was free to redirect thousands of men in Virginia, including General George Pickett's regiments, to the northern campaign in Pennsylvania.

Lee needed soldiers, too. His hard-fighting Army of Northern Virginia was shrinking in size, despite strong efforts to sign up more men, and this troubled him. How long could his men stay on the field and fight?

There was a political masterstroke Lee hoped to add to the invasion. He read as many Northern newspapers as he could find, as did his generals, and they all reported a growing peace movement in the North, made up of tens of thousands of residents of the Northern states who wanted Lincoln to end the war and let the Confederacy remain as its own country. A Confederate victory in Pennsylvania, or wherever the two armies met, would give the peace movement people a very strong reason to howl even louder.

One thing that did not trouble him, and should have, was the early and strenuous objections to any invasion of the North by General James Longstreet, now his No. 2 man. Longstreet did not want to invade anywhere. He wanted the Union troops to come to a battle with the Southerners, where they would be defeated. Longstreet's foreboding feeling had been there since mid-May and would grow and grow until Pickett's Charge. Lee, however, incorrectly assumed Longstreet agreed with his overall plan.

As he rode for Pennsylvania, Lee had lost his famous cavalry commander General J. E. B. Stuart. He had authorized Stuart to ride around Hooker's army to gather information, but none was forthcoming. Where on earth was Stuart? What neither Stuart nor Lee knew was that Hooker's entire army had crossed the Potomac and headed for Pennsylvania, where Lee himself was headed. He did not know where Hooker was, though, nor the size of his force, because he had no reports from Stuart.

Lee's large army, without word from Stuart, hoped to clash with the Federals, but it did not know much about their size or position. With Stuart's disappearance, Lee and his forces were playing a game of blindman's bluff as they rode north and approached a tiny village called Gettysburg.

PART ONE
The Road to Gettysburg

The Civil War was two years old in 1863 when General Robert E. Lee told president of the Confederacy Jefferson Davis (who was running the seceded South from his office in a converted mansion in Richmond, Virginia) that he wanted to invade the North a second time to strike a stinging blow at the Federal forces and win the war. If Lee got into Pennsylvania, he could take the bustling state capital, Harrisburg, seize the busy railroads there, put his troops on the trains, and quickly ride into downtown Philadelphia and claim victory. The Liberty Bell would ring again.

If that path failed, Lee could get his men on the rumbling trains again and, unannounced, ride an hour or so farther east across the farmlands of New Jersey into New York City. Surprised, hardworking New Yorkers, so used to the idea that the Civil War was very, very far away from them and their families, would cause a huge uproar at their sudden defeat and the occupation of America's largest city. There would be thousands of angry and stunned New Yorkers streaming through the streets of the city in inflamed and lengthy protest marches.

The invasion would also be a public relations blow that would shake the North to its core. How could such a thing possibly happen? Northerners would be astounded that an invading army, especially one that large—72,000 men—could get all the way to New York. They would wonder why New York City had absolutely no defense against an invasion and, most of all, why continue a war in which New York, and apparently any Northern city, could so easily be attacked and occupied? They would be so shocked that they would force President Abraham Lincoln to surrender and grant the South its recently claimed status as a new nation representing half of what had been the United States. Would this, indeed, be the end of the Union?

At the very least, Lee claimed an invasion of the North could help both the military and public image of the Confederate Army.

General Robert E. Lee

Valuable results might be expected to follow a decided advantage gained over the enemy in Maryland and Pennsylvania, too.

Lee and President Davis were friends. They became friends when Davis was the US secretary of war in the 1850s and Lee was the commandant at the United States Military Academy at West Point. The two men not only respected each other, but also liked each other. Lee had a special place in his heart for Davis because Davis had been a hero for the US Army in the Mexican War (1846–1848). Most secretaries of war were strictly political appointees, but not Jeff Davis. Davis, a Mississippian, had been in the middle of a savage war in Mexico and had, as a young man, shown extraordinary courage and leadership skills. In the war, Davis had given himself a short course on leadership in the US Army. What did he do in the Black Hawk War? He captured Chief Black Hawk. From a soldier's point of view, Davis was the perfect military president. Northerners? They had Abraham Lincoln, whose major military skill over the years was not leading an army but splitting rails out in Illinois.

Davis and Lee got along splendidly. One of Davis's most self-gratifying acts as president of the Confederacy, in fact, was appointing Lee the commander of the Army of Northern Virginia—the home state of his new general.

Virginians seemed to have the upper hand in the Confederate Army, and that did cause some antagonism and jealousy. Many complained that too many Virginians were in charge of the army, and the Virginians in charge of it complained that there were not enough Virginians in it. **General Lafayette McLaws** wrote to his old friend from West Point, General Richard Ewell:

General Lafayette McLaws
Do you know there is a strong feeling growing among the Southern troops against Virginia, caused by the jealousy of her own people for those from every other state? No matter who it is may perform a glorious act, Virginia papers give but a grudging praise unless the actor is a Virginian. No matter how trifling the deed may be which a Virginian performs, it is heralded at once as the most glorious of modern times.

But Lee, himself, was widely admired both inside and outside the army.

Mary Chesnut, Southern diarist
General Lee, son of Light Horse Harry Lee, has been made general in chief of Virginia. With such men to the fore, we have hope.

Lee, for his part, said the new Confederacy would have a hard job of selling itself. He knew war was bleeding and dying, not parades and social teas, as most Southerners seemed to believe. He told John Imboden, a Virginia legislator and Confederate general:

General Robert E. Lee
I fear our people do not yet realize the magnitude of the struggle they have entered upon, nor its probable duration and the sacrifices it will impose upon them. The United States government is one of the most powerful upon earth. I know the people and the government we will have to

contend with. In a little while, they will be even more united than we are. Their resources are almost without limit. Their army . . . will be commanded by the foremost soldier of the country, General [Winfield] Scott. . . . And above all, we shall have to fight the prejudices of the world, because of the existence of slavery in our country.

Lee was also disappointed in the reluctance of his friends and neighbors in Virginia to rally to the precious cause, as he himself had done. He shook his head when discussing them.

General Robert E. Lee
They are worse than children.

Lee continued to shake his head when he led his first troops in South Carolina. People in that state, too, were reluctant to wave their new flag and cheer their new army.

General Robert E. Lee
I am dreadfully disappointed at the spirit here. The people do not seem to realize there is a war. It is so very hard to get anything done [here]. . . . While we all wish well and mean well, it is so difficult to get them to act energetically and promptly. Our people have not been in earnest enough to have thought too much of themselves and their ease & instead of turning out to a man, they have been content to nurse themselves & their dimes & leave the protection of themselves and families to others.

Over the past two years, the combination of Davis and Lee had not brought victory overall in the war, but it had brought victory in numerous battles in several states. What the two men needed now, in the spring and summer of 1863, was a huge win over the Union's best army, the Army of Potomac, commanded since January that year by General Joseph "Fighting Joe" Hooker.

Another problem Lee's army had was food. He had just about taken all the available food in northern Virginia and every day needed more. A successful invasion of Pennsylvania and its thousands of acres of productive farmland would enable him to get badly needed supplies for his soldiers, not only for this campaign, but others in the future.

Until now, President Lincoln had been let down by just about all his generals. The Union forces won some battles and so did the Confederates, but the bloody war droned on. Everyone was tired of it. Soldiers began sniping at their officers. One target was the meticulously attired Union general Winfield Scott, who was criticized for wearing a different white shirt every day.

Lieutenant Colonel Theodore Lyman, Union Army
Where he gets them, no one knows.

Lincoln's prize, the prize of the army, the prize of all the North, was flamboyant General George McClellan. McClellan, never known for humility, wrote that the people saw him as some kind of a god on a horse.

General George McClellan, Union Army
The people call on me to save the country. I must save it and cannot respect anything that is in my way.

People had told Lincoln that the immaculately dressed McClellan, who looked so fit and proper on his horse and had a commanding style about him, was the best possible choice to be commanding general of the US Army.

He was not.

Lincoln also did not know the disdain McClellan had for him.

General George McClellan
President Lincoln is the original gorilla . . . an idiot.

Lincoln removed McClellan as commanding general of the Union Army in March 1862, but left him at the head of the Army of the Potomac—responsible for military and naval operations in Virginia, West Virginia, Maryland, Pennsylvania, Washington, DC, and the coastal fortifications and seaports of North Carolina. Then he fumbled badly at a major battle at Antietam, Maryland, in September of 1862. After the general failed to pursue Lee's army in Maryland, the president rode to McClellan's home in Washington to discuss the war with him. He did not have an appointment.

General George McClellan, to his servant
Tell Lincoln to go home.
Servant
It's the president.
General George McClellan
He has no appointment with me.
Servant
It's the president. . . .
General George McClellan
Tell him to go home.

Soon after that, Lincoln fired McClellan entirely.

He was replaced at the head of the Army of Potomac by General Ambrose E. Burnside, who lasted just three months. Then came Hooker.

General Henry Halleck became commanding general after McClellan in July 1862, but no one brought the president victory. In fact, few in the army or the Lincoln administration thought very much of Commanding General Henry Halleck.

Secretary of the Navy Gideon Welles
[Halleck] originates nothing, anticipates nothing . . . takes no responsibility, plans nothing, suggests nothing, is good for nothing.

Lincoln told all the generals of all his armies that his goal was a speedy victory, not a long, slow string of battles. Lincoln wanted to end this war; he had to end this war.

President Abraham Lincoln
Neither party expected for the war, the magnitude or the duration, which it has already attained.

General Oliver Otis Howard, Union Army
We cannot well exaggerate . . . the horrors, hateful ravages, and the countless expense of war.

To be victorious, President Lincoln told his commanders, they had to crush the Confederate armies, not spend time capturing their cities. Hooker should have crushed his foes at Chancellorsville in the spring of 1863, but they fought on. McClellan should have crushed his foes at Antietam, but he did not—and yet he bragged about his "victory." The Battle of Antietam wound up as a draw and it angered Lincoln that McClellan painted it as his personal victory.

Some men worried at the small size of the Union Army. Others wrung their hands at the need for any army.

Horace Greeley, Editor, *New-York Tribune*
Of all solecisms, a Standing Army in a Republic of the XIX century is the most indefensible. We have no more need of a standing army than of an order of nobility.

The armies both sides put together often had no skill in mapmaking, troop movements, or supplying a force of that size.

General Richard Taylor, Confederate Army

The Confederate commanders . . . were without maps, sketches, or proper guides and knew no more about the topography of the country than they did about Central Africa.

The United States Army had been a ragtag and disorderly operation for years. Winfield Scott, the highest-ranking US general in the Mexico War, said in 1847:

General Winfield Scott

Our militia and volunteers, if a tenth of what is said to be true, have committed atrocities—horrors—in Mexico, sufficient to make heaven weep, and every American, of Christian morals, blush for his country.

And the while Union and Confederate soldiers were being painted as "mortal enemies," most men in both the Northern and Southern forces didn't see it that way.

Lieutenant Colonel Thomas Hyde, Union Army

[We fight] in obedience to the dictates of duty and patriotism, not in personal hatred towards who for the time they call enemies.

Leonidas Torrence, 13th North Carolina, letter to his sister

If you were to see a yankey, you would think it was a man, too. They are nothing more than other men.

Spencer Cavendish, the Marquis of Hartington in Great Britain, toured the United States in August of 1862. He visited the headquarters of both armies and met with Presidents Abraham Lincoln and Jefferson Davis. He described the Southerners as tough and determined fighters.

The Marquis of Hartington

I have seen them serving as privates in regiments of their states, serving badly clothed, badly fed, perhaps hardly with shoes upon their feet. . . . I have seen men who have lived all their lives in poverty, who you would say have nothing to lose and nothing to gain, who had no interest in slavery, but who have joined with as much readiness as those who had the ranks of the army. I have seen these men in their camps as cheerful as possible, and asking for nothing but again to be led to battle with the enemy. . . . I say surely a people animated with such a feeling [are] not a people who are going to give in.

And then there were those who were born in the North but lived now in the South.

Harry Handerson, born in the North, moved to Louisiana

All my interests lay in the South, and with Southerners, and if the seceding states, one of which I resided in, chose deliberately to try the experiment of self-government, I felt quite willing to give them such aid as lay in my feeble power.

In the South, the small press corps was all behind General Lee and President Davis, while in the North the mainstream press was frustrated by the North's failure to gain a decisive victory and highly critical of Lincoln who, as president, was commander in chief of the army.

Lee stopped McClellan from taking Richmond in the spring and summer of 1862. But the Union sailed into and took the Southern stronghold of beautiful New Orleans, a strategic seaport, in that same year. Young General Ulysses S. Grant, a beloved "hard ass," won some battles in the West and Southerners took some in the East.

McClellan was replaced as the head of the Army of Potomac by General Ambrose E. Burnside, who lasted just three months. Then came Hooker. But shortly after Lee and Davis met, Lincoln happily accepted Hooker's resignation, and he was replaced on June 28, 1863, by the untested General George Meade.

Meade did not have much experience in battles against the best Southern armies. How would he do if he ever found himself on a field opposed by Lee?

Meade wrote to his wife about his promotion and what he knew would be a looming battle with Lee.

General George Meade, to his wife

As dearest, you know how reluctant we both have been to see me placed in this position, and it appears to be God's will for some good purpose—at any rate, as a soldier I had nothing to do but accept and exert my utmost abilities to command success. This, so help me God, I will do. And trusting to him, who in his good pleasure has thought proper to place me where I am, I shall pray for strength and power to get through with the task assigned me. . . . I am moving at once against Lee. Pray earnestly. Pray for the success of my country. Love to all!

Who was George Meade anyway? He was not a "fighter," like Fighting Joe Hooker. He was not a portrait of sartorial splendor and greatness, like George McClellan.

General Alpheus Williams, Union Army, to his daughter
Soldiers saw him as a tall, slim, grey-bearded man who wore glasses and an old slouched hat, a blue blouse, corduroy pants tucked into his long jackboots . . . ungainly in looks and actions.

Many who knew Meade simply did not like him.

Assistant Secretary of War Charles Dana
[Meade] was an intellectual man, and agreeable to talk with when his mind was free, but silent and indifferent to everybody when he was occupied with that which interested him. . . . He had the worst possible temper, especially towards his subordinates. I think he had not a friend in the whole army. He [cursed] them violently, without occasion and without reason . . . he lacked moral authority.

And so, many in the army said, your success with General Meade did not depend on your situation so much as his mood that day.

Lieutenant Colonel Theodore Lyman, Union Army
Meade was always stirring up somebody. This morning it was the cavalry picket line, which extends for miles and which he declared was ridiculously placed. But, by worrying, and flailing out unexpectedly, on various officers, he does manage to have things pretty shipshape.

On the other hand, when Meade did wrong to somebody, he always apologized.

Meade aide
[He had] a cordial desire to make amends.

Meade was a quiet man, almost aloof, but when he did talk to people he often wound up telling funny stories and jokes. The more he talked, the friendlier he became.

General Alexander Webb, Meade's chief of staff
He talked with great fluency and elegant language.

He was also a man of great strength and character.

Lieutenant Colonel Theodore Lyman
He has a tremendous nervous system [that holds him up] through everything. . . . [Meade is] a thorough soldier and a mighty clear-headed man and one who does not move unless he knows where and how many his men are, where and how many his enemy's men are and what sort of country he has to go through. I never met a man in my life who was so characterized by straightforward truthfulness as he is. He will pitch into himself in a moment if he thinks he had done wrong, and woe to those, no matter who they are, who do not do it right.

General Gouverneur Warren, Union Army
[At Gettysburg] Meade's moral character was a tower of strength to us and gave hope to the hearts of those who sought the favor of Providence and believed in the success of a just cause.

But perhaps the most impressive memorial to Meade was not from a soldier, but a civilian.

Frederick Law Olmsted, US Sanitary Commission
[He had] a most soldiery and veteran-like appearance, a grave, stern countenance, somewhat Oriental in its dignified expression, yet American in its

racehorse gauntness. He is simple, direct, deliberate and thoughtful in manner of speech and general address. . . . He is a gentleman and an old soldier.

If the newly appointed General Meade was not experienced in major victories, General Lee certainly was. His latest, over a major Union force, was at Chancellorsville, Virginia, about two months before Meade took up his new position. Lee had split his outnumbered troops in the face of Hooker's advance, and that daring move brought victory. Now, in the spring of 1863, Lee and his confident men were still celebrating the win at Chancellorsville, despite the accidental death of General Thomas "Stonewall" Jackson, who was hit by friendly fire.

Lee was certain that if he could find and defeat the Army of the Potomac—which he had just defeated at Chancellorsville—in Pennsylvania, he could win the war.

When Lee and Davis met, Hooker was still in charge, and he had few supporters in the Union Army.

General Alpheus Williams, Union Army

I cannot conceive of greater imbecility and weakness that characterized that campaign from the moment Hooker reached Chancellorsville and took command.

Referring to Hooker, General Alexander Webb wrote his father:

General Alexander Webb, Union Army

[Our generals] are contemptible blocks with stars on their shoulders [who] in moments of trial have asked me what to do! How to do it! & look like sheep when they ought to show character. This is known to all and yet you see no improvement in the appointments.

And Hooker was not the only general who was widely disliked in the Union Army.

General Marsena Patrick, Union Army

[General Daniel Butterfield] seems to be held in universal contempt yet is regarded with more than loathing by those who feel his power.

General Andrew Humphreys, Union Army

[Butterfield] is false, treacherous, and cowardly.

Colonel Lucius Fairchild, Union Army, letter to his sister

[I am so disgusted with the service that] I was almost ready to resign. [When I thought of the] many Generals under whom I had a chance to be thrown—political Generals who are perfect failures, Generals who are drunkards, Generals who are not fit for the places they hold—I get a big disgust on. When I see the reputation of a good regiment resting on the reports of popinjay staff officers who would not make first class corporals—then I get mad as the d——l and swear some.

Hooker always claimed that he had actually won a victory at Chancellorsville, and argued with those who thought otherwise. He wrote to his friend Samuel Bates:

General Joseph Hooker

You may like to know my opinion of the Battle of Chancellorsville so far as my individual efforts were concerned, and I had no hesitation in giving it to you. I won greater success in many fields of the war, but nowhere did I deserve I half so much [credit] and when all of the records [North and South] are correctly published, I believe [my victory] will be conceded by all of my countrymen.

But Lincoln was devastated by the loss to Lee at Chancellorsville.

President Abraham Lincoln, on the defeat at Chancellorsville
My God! My God! What will the nation say?

Spirits were low in the Union Army after the defeat. In late May 1863, a Union soldier wrote:

Union soldier, 142nd Pennsylvania
No bright spark seems to arise. . . . All is dark and gloomy.

Horace Greeley, Editor, *New-York Tribune*
Unquestionably, the first six months of 1863 were the darkest hours of the national cause.

But Lee told colleagues and friends that he never felt triumphant about Chancellorsville. It was a victory, yes, but one like that at Fredericksburg, it did not advance the Confederate Army. It meant little in the long run.

The South was moving too slowly, Lee believed, and needed a successful invasion of the North not just for military success, but as a public relations coup.

General Robert E. Lee
At Chancellorsville, we gained another victory—our people were wild with delight—I, on the contrary, was more depressed than after Fredericksburg. Our loss was severe and, again, we had gained not an inch of ground and the enemy could not be pursued.

The South, Lee was more and more convinced each day, needed to invade the North. He and his generals had taken steps already to make that happen. Before his death, Stonewall Jackson had asked the

Confederate's chief mapmaker, Jedediah Hotchkiss, to draw a map showing a good path for the Southern army from the hills of northern Virginia to Harrisburg, the capital of Pennsylvania, and then on to Philadelphia. Now Lee had that map.

Southerners rallied behind Lee. Most of them wanted an independent country, and in Lee (and also in President Davis), they saw an opportunity for that. After all, they all said, did not the United States do the same thing in fighting the American Revolution and separating from their mother country, Britain? Was not George Washington a hero in both North and South for leading the Revolutionary Army? There was no difference, Southerners said. They all put their faith in General Lee.

Lee also believed that a great victory over the US forces in an invasion of the North would convince both Britain and France to enter the war on the Confederate side. European troops, ships, cannons, and money would help bring victory to the South. Their participation would also cast suspicion on the Lincoln government. Why would two world superpowers choose the South over the North?

By late June 1863, the North knew from rumors spread by reliable sources that the South was planning a major invasion of the North. It was not a surprise. President Lincoln had even met with Governor Andrew Curtin of Pennsylvania warning him that a Southern army was on its way into his state, either in late June or early July. The president did not know its size or its destination, but he warned the governor to get ready for it. So, on June 12 (three weeks before what turned out to be the Battle of Gettysburg), Curtin issued a proclamation warning Pennsylvanians of the South's certain attack and asking them to prepare.

Efforts to mobilize a state militia in Pennsylvania failed. Worse, different groups in the state believed the attack would come at different places. In Philadelphia, residents pleaded with Secretary of War Edwin Stanton to give them fifty cannon to protect the city and a railroad train big enough to transport 20,000 troops to anywhere in the state they were needed—immediately.

When, several weeks later, the famished Rebels did march into Maryland and Pennsylvania, they were happy to realize that they could buy food and other goods that had just about vanished in the South. They could also buy—or take—beer in Northern taverns. Union soldiers did the same thing. Hundreds of troops on both sides wound up drunk and a disgrace to their officers.

Union soldier, on his drunken friends
I never saw such a set in my life.

The Confederates were just as bad, but not as public. Their "valor" drew the attention of General Lee, who applauded his men while denouncing the Union soldiers.

General Robert E. Lee denounced . . .
. . . barbarous outrages upon the unarmed and defenseless and the wanton destruction of private property, that have marked the course of the enemy in our own country.

Despite Lee's comments, and similar comments by Union generals, local citizens in southern Pennsylvania all complained of soldiers from both sides stealing goods, general theft, and robberies.

General Lee and President Davis agreed that a successful invasion into the North could strengthen public opinion and win the war. After all, both men believed that small armies led by daring generals could always defeat large armies led by dull, by-the-book generals. That had happened in the Revolution, and they were convinced it would happen again here in the Civil War. George Washington had done it and now so would Robert E. Lee.

Southerners, from Davis and Lee right down to local farmers, had a dim view of the strength and skill of the Union Army, despite its enormous size and massive cannon firepower.

General Robert E. Lee

They [the Union Army] will come up probably through Frederick, broken down with hunger and hard marching. I shall throw an overwhelming force on their advance, crush it, follow up on the success, drive one corps on another, and by successive repulses and surprises, before they can concentrate, create a panic.

Also like Washington, Lee was a modest man. He was not a flamboyant dresser, like J. E. B. Stuart. He wore a plain soldier's hat and did not show off any awards or medals. You knew who he was by the three simple general's stars on his collar, by the beautiful white horse (named Traveler) he rode—and by his actions. He was a fine specimen of a soldier, tough as nails. Everybody, North and South, agreed on that.

Reporter, *Richmond Dispatch*, on Lee

No man is superior in all that constitutes a soldier and the gentleman—no man more worthy to head our forces and lead our army.

Lee was a graduate of West Point and had been a star, admired by all, during the Mexican War.

General Winfield Scott, during the Mexican War

Lee is the greatest soldier now living and if he ever gets the opportunity he will prove himself the greatest captain of history.

General Winfield Scott, to the secretary of war in 1857

Lee was the very best soldier I ever saw in the field.

As a Southern general, Lee's only shortcoming was that he was opposed to slavery.

General Robert E. Lee, in 1856

In this enlightened age, there are few, I believe, but what will acknowledge that slavery, as an institution, is amoral and political evil in any country.

He did not believe violence was the way to end it, though; he believed that it would pass from the nation's doorstep peacefully in a few years, without any need for war.

Initially, he also held little regard for the Confederate cause and its army.

General Robert E. Lee, letter to his son

When this war began, I was opposed to it, bitterly opposed to it. And I told these people that unless every man should do his whole duty, they would repent it.

General Lee became commander of the Confederate Army in June 1862, after the Battle of Seven Pines, near Richmond, when General Joseph E. Johnston was badly wounded. Those in the Army liked Lee immediately. Porter Alexander, a Confederate artillery officer who eventually rose to the rank of brigadier general, related what a fellow soldier told him when he wondered whether Lee could lead an army.

Confederate soldier

Alexander, if there is one man in either army, federal or Confederate, who is, head and shoulders, far above every other one in either army in audacity, that man is General Lee. . . . that man is audacity personified.

Colonel John Mosby, Confederate Army cavalry battalion commander
Lee was the most aggressive man I met in the war and was always ready for any enterprise.

Jefferson Davis agreed.

President Jefferson Davis
Lee's natural temper was combative.

A British journalist who observed Lee at the Battle of the Wilderness, an intense engagement fought in dense woods, wrote about Lee:

British journalist
No man who, at the terrible moment, saw his flashing eyes and sternly set lips is ever like to forget them . . . or the light of battle, flaming in his eyes.

Lee fought off a Union invasion of Virginia in 1862, had victories around Richmond at Mechanicsville, Gaines' Mill, Savage's Station, Frayser's Farm, and Malvern Hill, and successfully chased the bluecoats out of the area. He then began to plan an invasion of the North but was hurt by his own disorganized force and resistance by the Union Army under General McClellan.

Now, in 1863, with the full support of President Davis, he wanted to try again. This time he sincerely believed that a stunning attack on the North, with many victories, would force Lincoln to seek a negotiated peace with the South and sanction their new country.

He thought all these things because he believed he was in command of a solid, formidable army that he believed to be invincible.

General Robert E. Lee
There were never such men in an army before. They will go anywhere and do anything if properly led.

Following the death of Stonewall Jackson, Lee picked General James "Old Pete" Longstreet as his second in command. Longstreet was the soldier's soldier, a tough guy, and Lee liked him.

General James Longstreet, at the Battle of Antietam in 1862, to General Roger Atkinson Pryor
This is a hard fight and we had better all die than lose it.

General Longstreet was a large man, a man of few words, and a man with good leadership skills. Many in the army admired him immensely.

Lieutenant Colonel Moxley Sorrel, aide to Longstreet at Manassas
A most striking figure . . . a soldier every inch and very handsome, tall and well proportioned, strong and active, a superb horseman and with an unsurpassed soldierly bearing, his features and expressions fairly matched; eyes glint steel blue, deep and piercing, a full brown beard, a head well shaped and poised. The worst feature was the mouth, rather coarse. It was partially hidden, however, by his ample beard.

Lieutenant William Pettit, Confederate Army
Lt. General Longstreet wore a gray military coat and pants, the coat with remarkable short skirts or tail. It was a frock coat, of course, and did not

reach the middle of his thighs. He wore the same every day. He wore a gray or lead colored shawl wrapped closely around his neck and shoulders and kept in place by holding it together with his hands and arms, which were generally wrapped up in it. No marks of insignia or rank were visible. His hat was plain black felt, with rather narrow brim and high crown. A plain sword hung at his side. He is about six feet, two inches high, with a strong round frame, portly and fleshy but not corpulent or too fat. His hair is dark auburn and long. His whiskers and moustache are the same color and thick and heavy. His forehead is broad and full. His brows are heavy, his nose is straight and rather fleshy and his eyes, which are set in close to his nose, are dark and steady in their movements and gaze. The lips come quite close together. He is about 190 pounds. He is almost always walking to and fro, except when gazing upon the battlefield, his shawl hugged closely about his neck and shoulders, apparently intensely thinking. He spoke but seldom, and then in low tone. He had a very intellectual appearance, is certainly a very industrious man and an energetic, skillful officer. Next to Lee, I should entrust the chief command of our army to him.

Lieutenant Thomas Goree, on Longstreet's staff, agreed.

Lieutenant Thomas Goree, Confederate Army

General Longstreet is one of the kindest, best hearted men I have ever known. Those not acquainted with him think him short and crabbed and he does appear so except in three places—First, when in the presence of ladies, second at the table, third, on the field of battle. At any one of these places he has a complacent smile on his countenance, and seems to be one of the happiest men in the world.

Longstreet had great stamina and energy and went most nights with just a few hours' sleep. (He often paced back and forth when he could not sleep.)

General James Longstreet, Confederate Army
I have never felt fatigue in my life.

Arthur Fremantle, British journalist
The iron endurance of General Longstreet is most extraordinary; he seems to require neither food nor sleep.

General Longstreet was also concerned about the health and welfare of others. For example, in October 1862 he wrote General Joseph Johnston, newly appointed to command the Department of the West, and offered to take Johnston's men west himself because Johnston seemed ill.

General James Longstreet
I can't become reconciled to your going west to command the 1st corps in this army. If you will take it, you are more than welcome to it, and I have no doubt the command of the entire army will fall to you before spring. . . . If it is possible for me to relieve you by going west, don't hesitate to send me. It would put me into no great inconvenience. On the contrary, it will give me pleasure if I can relieve you of it. I fear you ought not to go where you will be exposed to the handicaps that you will meet . . . there. I am entirely sound and believe I can endure anything.

Longstreet never saw himself as the commander of anything, but as a solid and good lieutenant to his boss, Lee.

General James Longstreet, to Lee
I know that it is the habit in all armies to represent their own positions as the most important ones. And it may be that this feeling is operating with me, but I am not prompted by any desire to do, or attempt to do,

great things. I only wish to do what I regard as my duty—give you the full benefit of my views.

Arthur Fremantle, British journalist
Longstreet is never far from Lee, who relies very much upon his judgment.

After the war, Longstreet wrote about what he believed Lee expected of him.

General James Longstreet
[Lee] always invited my views in moves of strategy and general policy, not so much for the purpose of having his own views approved and confirmed as to get new lights, or channels, for new thought, and was more pleased when he found something that gave him new strength than with efforts to evade his questions with compliments. When oppressed by severe study, he sometimes sent for me to say that he had applied himself so closely to a matter that he found his ideas running around in a circle and was in need of help to find a tangent.

The problem with Longstreet, Lee knew, was that he was thin-skinned and did not take orders well. Several months later, Goree was critical of his boss in a letter to his family in Texas.

Lieutenant Thomas Goree, Confederate Army
At home with his staff, he is some days social and agreeable. Then again for a few days he will confine himself mostly to his room or tent without having much to say to anyone and is as grim as you please, although when this is the case he is usually not very well or something has not gone to suit him. When anything has gone wrong he does not say very much but merely looks grim.

We all know how to take him and do not now talk to him without, we find, he is in a talkative mood. He had a good deal of the roughness of the old soldier about him, more, I think, than either Generals Johnston, Beauregard, Van Dorn or Smith.

Still, Lee and Longstreet became friendly and the two men often pitched their headquarters tents next to each other. Men would walk by the tents just to see their leaders. Sir Arthur Fremantle, a British military officer and journalist who visited the United States during the Civil War and witnessed the Battle of Gettysburg, noted that soldiers would also walk or ride ahead of their regiment to get a look at their general.

Arthur Fremantle, British journalist

As they have nearly always been on detached duty, few of them [Southern soldiers] knew General Longstreet, except by reputation. Numbers of them asked me whether the General in front was Longstreet; and when I answered in the affirmative, many would run on a hundred yards in order to take a good look at him. This I take to be an immense compliment from any soldier on a long march.

Lee also had General Richard Ewell and General John Gordon with him on the advance into Pennsylvania. In an era when appearances mattered a great deal, Ewell was an oddity, with his large eyes and nearly bald head. He also questioned many orders from Longstreet. Gordon did not have a military background, but he did have good instincts. Before the Battle of Gettysburg, Gordon declared that whichever army claimed Cemetery Ridge would win the battle. He was right.

The Southern people were all behind General Lee and his army. A reception for Lee and General J. E. B. Stuart in Culpeper, Virginia, in 1863 was evidence of that. Heros von Borcke (a Prussian cavalry officer who served as a Confederate cavalry officer in the Army of Northern Virginia) wrote about the event.

Heros von Borcke

Every train that afternoon brought in fresh crowds of our guests and we all assembled at the station to receive them and forward them to their destinations by the ambulances and wagons we had prepared for that purpose. In the evening, there was a ball at the town hall, which went off pleasantly enough, although it was not . . . a gay and dazzling scene illuminated by a flood of light streaming from numerous chandeliers, our supply of light was limited to a few tallow candles, and when the moon rose we were glad to avail ourselves by adjourning to the spacious veranda. . . . [W]e completed our preparations and gave the last touch to our arms and equipment, and about eight o'clock General Stuart and his staff mounted their horses and made for the plains of Brandy Station. Our little band presented a gay and gallant appearance as we rode forth to the sound of our bugles all mounted on fine chargers and dressed in our best accouterments, our plumes nodding and our battle flags waving.

The horse on which I was mounted seemed to me in the very perfection of beauty as it danced the springing step upon the turf, its glossy coat shining like burnished gold in the morning sun.

About ten o'clock the marching commenced. General Stuart had taken his position on a slight eminence, wither many hundreds of spectators, mostly ladies, had gathered in ambulances and on horseback anxiously awaiting the approach of the troops. The corps passed by squadrons, and at a walk, and the magnificent spectacle of so many thousands of troopers so splendidly mounted made the heart swell with pride and impressed . . . the conviction that nothing [could stop] the attack of such a body of troops. . . . [At night] we danced in the open air on a piece of turf near our headquarters and by the light of enormous woodfires, the steady glare of which upon the animated groups of our assembly gave to the whole scene a wild and romantic effect.

All there enjoyed the reception and the day.

General Robert E. Lee

The men and horses looked well. . . . Stuart was in all his glory. . . . The country here looks very green and pretty, notwithstanding the ravages of war. What a beautiful world God in his loving kindness to his creatures has given us!

Lee's opinion about the pretty countryside was shared by Heros von Borcke and all the soldiers, North and South. They were always amazed at the physical beauty of the places where bloody battles were fought.

Heros von Borcke

Our tents were pitched in a beautiful spot, overshadowed by magnificent hickory and tulip-poplar trees, and surrounded by broad clover fields, where our horses were richly pastured and through which the pretty little river, Mountain Run, rolled its silver waters between picturesque banks and afforded us the chance of a magnificent cool bath and plenty of sport with the rod and line. Our cavalry were in the highest spirits and were kept in constant and salutary activity by incessant drilling and other preparations for the impending campaign.

In the engagement they marched off to from Culpeper, the Confederate cavalry clashed with General Hooker at nearby Brandy Station on June 9, 1863. The South fought evenly with the 9,500 men under the legendary Stuart, who had won numerous victories in the first two years of the war and earned a tremendous reputation.

The Union cavalry was commanded by General Alfred Pleasonton. In the end, neither side gained much after fourteen hours of hard fighting. But it proved that the North's cavalry was just as good as the South's.

Colonel John Mosby, Confederate Army
[Union General Alfred Pleasonton] went after a fight. . . .

Stuart and his men claimed victory at Brandy Station.

Lieutenant Colonel W. W. Blackford, on Stuart's staff
By all the tests recognized for war, victory was fairly ours. We captured three cannon and 500 prisoners, and held the field.

So did Pleasonton and his men.

General Alfred Pleasonton, Union Army
The rebels are like that boy the President [Lincoln] described who stumped his toe and was too big to cry.

Lieutenant Colonel William Brooke Rawle, Union Army
We leisurely withdrew across the river unmolested. . . . I state positively that Confederate claims that they pursued us across the river are incorrect.

The engagement was the biggest cavalry battle ever fought in North America, and it made it clear to Union General Hooker that General Lee had a very large army. So Hooker started adding men and weapons to his own force. He planned to move a mass of troops to the Richmond area to crush the Southern army there, and then move to Richmond to take it and win the war. But President Lincoln stopped him.

In the spring and summer of 1863, a frustrated Lincoln ignored statistics that showed the North, with Meade's army, had about 105,000 men and the South in Lee's army just 75,000 or so (studies showed that Hooker's real strength was about 78,000 men, much closer to Lee's army size). It might have been an easy victory for the North if they could trap Lee somewhere, anywhere, somehow.

President Lincoln did not want any of the armies that protected Washington moving to Virginia to take on Stuart or anyone else—leaving Washington open to attack by Confederates. He told Hooker in no uncertain terms that he did not want any of his armies crossing any of the rivers into the South.

President Abraham Lincoln

In case you find Lee coming to the north of the Rappahannock [River] I would by no means cross to the South.

In mid-June, Hooker "demanded" an additional 25,000 men to engage Lee. Lincoln denied the request and told Hooker to do the best he could with his already quite large army of 105,000.

While all this was going on, Lee, with the full support of President Davis and his cabinet, headed into Maryland with his eye on Maryland and southwestern Pennsylvania. He told some people that thousands of men in Maryland would join his army when it marched through the state, inflating its size and power.

They did not.

When Hooker learned that Lee and his some 75,000 men had successfully crossed the wide waters of the Potomac River and were happily camping in Maryland, he ordered all his men to cross the Potomac as well. But it was the wrong time of the year. It was hot—blazing hot—when the Union forces made the crossing. Hundreds fell from their horses or collapsed while marching under the incredibly hot sun.

General Lee was genuinely surprised when he heard Hooker had crossed the Potomac. He had scouts in the area that reported the whereabouts and movements of Hooker's army, and Lee should have known Hooker's men, like his own, were headed somewhere in Pennsylvania. He blamed General Stuart.

General Robert E. Lee

[Loss of cavalry at Brandy Station] made it impossible to obtain accurate information or to ascertain the enemy's intentions.

After the war, Stuart wrote a report on the Gettysburg campaign in which he held himself blameless. Confederate general Wade Hampton read it and did not agree.

General Wade Hampton, Confederate Army

Lately, I saw for the first time Stuart's report of the Gettysburg campaign and I never read a more erroneous—to call it no harsher name—one than it was.

Lee's men, now in Maryland, had good things and bad things happen to them, sometimes at the same time. W. C. Ward, a Confederate private, described one victory/defeat—a rather personal one.

Private W. C. Ward, 4th Alabama

The rain still falling . . . the commissary department, with whiskey . . . undertook to wet the inside of the tired, hungry and wet soldiers by distributing about one half gil to each man. It was good whiskey and we had not had any for many months. Knowing how good such a stimulant was at the end of a hard day's march, this private soldier attempted to do a prudent thing. Instead of pouring his whiskey into his stomach, he turned it into his canteen. The march was resumed and after moving rapidly northward for about one hour the division was halted to rest. All lay down on the roadside, wet though it was, and when we rose again to resume the march the canteen in which the whiskey had been so carefully poured had been reversed and all that soldier's good spirits lost.

But not all the Confederates were doing "prudent things."

Colonel William C. Oates, 15th Alabama

We marched into Pennsylvania that afternoon and went into camp before night [south of Greencastle]. I, with adjutant Waddell, rode out into the country and found some of the soldiers committing depredations on the Dutch farmers, which I promptly rebuked, and ordered the men to camps wherever we found them. This was done in obedience to General Lee's order forbidding interference with private property because it was wrong and should never be done, even in an enemy's country, except when absolutely necessary. But, as far as I saw, these depredations extended only to taking something to eat and burning fenced rails for fuel. Some men would do this when they had plenty of rations in camp. At one house, we found some of our regiments milking the cows and catching the milk in canteens, which seemed to be very expert work of that kind. The people, as far as I could learn, seemed very alarmed but behaved well. Waddell and myself took supper that night with some people very loyal to the Union.

The Dutch women whom the Confederates met did not really know who to support, but their actions seemed to suggest to the Rebels that they supported the South.

James Hodam, 17th Virginia Cavalry

As we march along [toward Gettysburg], the women and children would stand at the front gate with large loaves of bread and a crock of apple butter and effectually prevent an entrance of the premises by the gray invaders. As I said before, the women could not talk much with us, but they knew how to provide "cut and smear" as the boys called it, in abundance.

The cherry crop was immense through this part of the state and the great [cherry] trees often overhung the highway laden with ripened fruit. The infantry would break off great branches and devour the cherries as they marched along. Regiments thus equipped reminded them of the scene in "Macbeth" where "Birnam wood remove to Dunsinane."

On one road the Confederates met a delightful pair of young women.

Confederate soldier

There were two young ladies in the family, and they, in common with the men of the household, conversed very freely after I assured them of their perfect right to speak their real sentiments. One of the ladies said that she wished the two armies would hang the two Presidents, Jefferson Davis and Abraham Lincoln, and stop the war. These people, although educated in books of some kind and apparently well informed on everything else, were remarkably ignorant of the causes of the war and real character [of the Confederate government]. They looked upon the war as a contention between two ambitious men for the supremacy, and were particularly spiteful towards Davis because they seem to think he wanted to dissolve the Union merely to be the President of the Southern Confederacy.

When the army of Confederate General John Gordon arrived in York, Pennsylvania, they expected a hostile reception. But that's not what they found.

General John Gordon, Confederate Army

We entered the city of York on Sunday morning, June 28. A committee composed of the Mayor and a committee of prominent citizens met my command on the main pike before we reached the corporate limits, their object being to make a peaceable surrender and ask for protection of life and property. They returned, I think, with a feeling of assured safety.

The church bells were ringing and the streets were filled with well-dressed people. The appearance of these men, women, and children in their Sunday attire strangely contrasted with that of my marching soldiers. Begrimed as we were, head to foot, with the impalpable gray powder which rose in dense columns from the macadamized pikes and settled in sheets on men, horses and wagons, it is no wonder that many of York's residents were terror-stricken as they looked upon us. We had been compelled on these forced marches to leave baggage wagons behind us and there was no possibility of a change of clothing, and no time for brushing uniforms or washing the disfiguring dust from faces, hair or beard. All these were the same hideous hue. . . . The grotesque aspect of my troops was accentuated here and there, too, by barefooted men mounted double on huge horses with shaggy manes and long fetlocks.

Confederate pride, to say nothing of Southern gallantry, was subjected to the sorest trial by the consternation produced among the ladies of York. In my eagerness to relieve the citizens from all apprehension, I lost sight of the fact that this turnpike powder was no respecter of persons, but that it enveloped all alike—officers as well as privates. . . . Halting on the main street, where the sidewalks were densely packed, I rode a few rods in advance of my troops, in order to speak to the people from my horse. As I checked him and turned my dust-begrimed face upon a bevy of young ladies very near me, a cry of alarm came from their midst. But after a few words of assurance from me, quiet and apparent confidence were restored. I assured these ladies that the troops behind me, though ill-clad and travel-stained, were good men and brave; that beneath their rough exteriors were hearts as loyal to women as ever beat in the breasts of honorable men; that their own experience, and the experience of their mothers, wives, and sisters at home, had taught them how painful must be the sight of a hostile army in their town and that under the orders of the commander in chief both private property and the spirit of vengeance and rapine had no place in the bosoms of these dust-covered but knightly men. And I closed by pledging to York the head of any soldier under my command who destroyed private property, disturbed the repose of a single home or insulted a woman.

Private W. C. Ward, Confederate Army

We were a merry lot. Entering the long, long streets of Greencastle [Pennsylvania] we found the people not at all afraid of us, as might have been expected.

While marching through Greencastle, Alabamian John Young took a hat off the head of an elderly gentleman and dropped it on the ground. Then he took off his own hat and dropped it next to the old man's. He put the old man's hat on his head and walked away. "I really believe that soldier has taken my hat," the old man said, watching forlornly as Young walked away and rejoined his regiment.

Private W. C. Ward

While going through Greencastle, the fife and drum of the 48th Alabama regiment played "The Bonnie Blue Flag." The doors of the houses were all closed but there was evidence of life in the upper stories. . . . We never halted. Marching through fields of newly planted corn and waving wheat, through orchards and currant bushes, we reached Chambersburg about noon. It was a beautiful town. Everything was fresh, indicating prosperity and no signs of war. . . . The stores were all closed and the men, bareheaded, were standing in front. To our laughing inquiry, "Where are your hats?" They replied laughing, "We have had some experience." There was nothing to indicate from the deportment of the citizens that their country was being invaded by a hostile army.

Passing out of Chambersburg by the northeast pike, as we went under a gateway under a hill crowned with a beautiful residence, we encountered many ladies, well dressed, bearing on their bosoms the Union flag . . . We took all of this in great good humor, neither giving or taking offense. . . . One of the young ladies, bolder than all the others, made a somewhat conspicuous and aggressive display of her flag and herself, accompanied by remarks. A bold Texan . . . said to the brave woman, "Madam, you are doing a very dangerous thing. . . . We rebels never see that flag flying over breastworks without charging them." The young woman made no reply but her companions had a good laugh at her expense. The Texan shouldered his [rifle] and went on his way, regretting that there were no orders to charge.

In Wrightsville, Pennsylvania, General Gordon and his men helped fight a fire sparked when the Yankees set fire to the nearby Columbia Bridge and shifting winds set the town ablaze. One woman invited a half dozen Southern soldiers to her home for breakfast in gratitude for saving her father's house from the fire.

General John Gordon

At a bountifully supplied table on the early morning sat this modest, cultured woman, surrounded by soldiers in their worn gray uniforms. The welcome she gave us was so gracious, she was so self-possessed, so calm, and kind, that I found myself in an inquiring state of mind as to whether her sympathies were with the Northern or Southern side in the pending war. Cautiously, but with sufficient clearance to indicate to her my object, I ventured with some remarks which she could not well ignore and which she saw were intended to evoke some declaration on the subject. She was too brave to evade it, too self-poised to be confused by it, and too firmly fixed in her convictions to hesitate as to the answer.

With no one present except Confederate soldiers, who were her guests, she replied, without a quiver in her voice, but with womanly gentleness, "General Gordon, I fully comprehend you, and it is due to myself that I candidly tell you that I am a Union woman. I cannot afford to be misunderstood, nor to have you misinterpret this simple courtesy. You and your soldiers last night saved my home from burning and I was unwilling that you should go away without receiving some token of my appreciation. I must tell you, however, that with my assent and approval, my husband is a soldier in the Union army and that my constant prayer to heaven is that our cause may triumph and the Union be saved."

No Confederate left that room without a feeling of profound respect, of unqualified admiration, for that brave and worthy woman.

As they advanced, the Southerners captured prisoners they did not want. One was a young drummer boy who was with a large group of captured soldiers.

James Hodam, Confederate Army

I met a large party of prisoners hurrying by, while a short distance behind them a little drummer boy was trying to keep up. He was bareheaded, wet and muddy, but still retained his drum.

"Hello my little Yank, and where are you going?"

"Oh," he said. "I am a prisoner and am going to Richmond."

"Look here," I said. "You are too little to be a prisoner, so pitch the drum near that fence corner, throw off your coat, get behind those bushes and go home as fast as you can."

"Mister, don't you want me for a prisoner?" he said.

"No."

"Can I go where I please?" the boy said.

"Yes," I answered.

"Then you bet I am going home to mother," he said, throwing his drum away and walking to some bushes and disappearing.

I sincerely hope he reached home and his mother.

Union General Hooker had recently asked for several thousand troops to be moved from Harpers Ferry, Virginia, to enlarge his already huge force.

General Joseph Hooker

I must have more men, [or else] my resignation.

Hooker thought his threat would force President Lincoln to send him the additional men. It did not. Lincoln again turned him down.

On June 28, 1863, Lee's army reached the Susquehanna River in Pennsylvania and Lincoln accepted Hooker's resignation as commander of the Army of the Potomac. To the astonishment of all, he named the newly promoted General George Meade (who was in Frederick, Maryland, at the time) as Hooker's replacement.

Although several officers had expressed a lack of confidence in Hooker, many in the Union Army criticized both the departure of Hooker and the timing of it, fearing that it would confuse things, with a confrontation in Pennsylvania clearly looming.

Colonel Thomas A. Scott, Assistant Secretary of War

It will cause delay in [the army's] movements and may prove fatal to Pennsylvania, as it gives the enemy time to overrun us and concentrate, if need be, in the heart of our state—or possibly it may enable Lee to crush the Army of the Potomac before the new commander finds out where his forces are.

Meade was forty-seven and looked older. He was a West Point graduate and a veteran of the Second Seminole War and the Mexican War. In 1862 he had been promoted to head of the Pennsylvania Reserves in the First Corps. He was widely respected.

Lieutenant Frank Haskell, Union Army

All thought highly of him. A man of great modesty, with none of those qualities which are noisy and assuming, and hankering for cheap newspaper fame. . . . I think my own notions concerning General Meade . . . were shared quite generally by the army. At all events, all who knew him shared them.

Lee also had enormous respect for Meade.

General Robert E. Lee

General Meade will commit no blunder in my front, and if I make one he will hasten to take advantage of it.

Three days after Meade's appointment, they both would have a chance to test Lee's prediction at Gettysburg.

When he took command, Meade had a pretty good, but not exact idea of where Lee was, and intended to move toward that area to attack Lee on his flank. Stopping Lee now, Lincoln and Meade knew, could end the war—if Meade could find Lee.

It seemed like everyone in Maryland and Pennsylvania knew where Lee's huge army was—except the Union soldiers, who had absolutely no clue where the Southerners were marching or where in Pennsylvania they were headed. As soon as the Confederates crossed the Potomac, signs in thick, smudgy, printed ink started to go up on thousands of trees and buildings announcing THE ENEMY IS APPROACHING and asking those in state militias to form their companies and march to where Lee's army was seen and prepare for battle against him.

Lee, too, lacked the information he needed—and made a very serious mistake. General Stuart, in charge of Lee's cavalry, had reconnoitered the passes through which the Union Army might pass in the Blue Ridge Mountains in Virginia. He wrote Lee a note saying that job was done and now he wanted to ramble around the area, keeping an eye on Meade's army while checking out more passes and roads.

Lee foolishly let him do so. He was famous, or infamous, for giving his commanders too much freedom. Lee was relying on Stuart for information on the armies of the North and South and where each was. Lee told Stuart:

General Robert E. Lee

If you find that [the enemy] is moving northward, and that two brigades can guard the Blue Ridge [mountains] & take care of your rear, you can move with the others . . . into Maryland & take a position on General

Ewell's right place. Keep yourself in communication with him, guard his flank, keep him informed of the enemy movements and collect all the supplies you can find for the use of the army.

Lee thought that was a precise and specific order, but Stuart did not. Stuart's reading of the message was to ride around, see what you can see, and let us know from time to time what you are doing. The impetuous Stuart, with his signature wide-brimmed hat and ever-growing beard, took off. He and his men left in a cloud of dust and were hardly heard from again—until they arrived very late at Gettysburg.

Lee did not hear from Stuart for more than a week and, nervous about his disappearance, begged anyone arriving at his camp to tell him where Stuart, and most of his entire cavalry, were. No one could. Lee fumed. There were no reports on Meade's army location and size. It was vital intelligence, and Lee needed it.

Lee decided to march to Cashtown, nine miles west of Gettysburg, from where he could get supplies, mass his troops, and start a march toward Harrisburg. But he had no idea where Meade and his huge army were, thanks to Stuart's disappearance. Lee was playing a military version of blindman's bluff.

As for Stuart, in his wanderings he ran into the rear guard of Union General Hugh J. Kilpatrick's cavalry division in the town of Hanover on June 30. Stuart attacked them, his men yelling and Stuart brandishing his sword.

E. A. Paul, *New York Times* reporter

General Stuart made a simultaneous attack upon his rear and right flank. The attack was entirely a surprise, as no enemy had been reported in the vicinity; and under any ordinary General, or less brave troops, so sudden and impetuous was the first charge, the whole command would have been thrown into the wildest confusion, and, as a necessary consequence, suffered a severe loss and a disastrous defeat. The force was in the hands of a master. Speedily making his dispositions, the Union captain,

General Elon Farnsworth, hurled upon the insolent and advancing enemy the Fifth New-York cavalry—a regiment never known to falter in an emergency.

For some time the contest hung in the balance, but General [George] Custer's brigade joined in, and after a severe struggle which lasted nearly four hours, the enemy was forced to retire. . . . Farnsworth was killed at Gettysburg.

A majority of the women in Hanover and elsewhere are truly loyal. They cared for the wounded—even taking them from the streets while bullets were flying around promiscuously. . . . A little boy named Smith, 12 years of age, who came out as bugler in the first Maine cavalry, was active in the fight, and had a horse killed under him at Hanover. Since that time he has been adopted as an aide by General Kilpatrick. . . .

Unnoticed at the end of the cavalry battle, Stuart did not head west to hook up with the other Southern generals, whose whereabouts he was familiar with. Instead, his army passed a girl's academy in Rockville, Maryland, where the girls were Rebel sympathizers. His soldiers were smitten.

Confederate Soldier

It was Sunday, and the beautiful girls in their fresh, gaily colored dresses, low necks, bare arms, and wilderness of braids and curls were "off duty" for the moment, and burning with enthusiasm to welcome the Southerner; for Rockville, in radical parlance, was a vile succession hole. Every eye flashed, every voice exclaimed, every rosy lip laughed, every fair hand waved a handkerchief or a sheet of music—smuggled—with crossed Confederate flags upon the cover. . . . As I drew near, . . . a beautiful girl of about sixteen rushed forth from the portico, pirouetting and clapping her hands in ecstasy at the sight of the gray uniform, exclaiming, "Oh, here is one of General Stuart's aides," and finished by pulling some hair from my calm and philosophical warhorse, on the expressly stated ground that he was a "secession" horse.

Then General Stuart approached with his column—gay, laughing, his blue eyes under the black feather full the joy. . . . [A] wild welcome greeted him.

Stuart did not tarry. In war, there is little time for gallant words, and news had just reached us from the front which moved the column on like the sound of a bugle—a mighty train of nearly 200 wagons, new, fresh painted, drawn by six mules each as became the Reserve Forage Train of the department at Washington had . . . approached from the East, intent on collecting forage. [Having been made aware of this,] they thundered back towards Washington. Stuart's face flushed at the thought of capturing the splendid prize and, shouting to a squadron to follow him . . . he went on a swift gallop on the track of the wagons.

Stuart went directly north—a path that would cause him to miss the start of the fight at Gettysburg, not arriving until late on the second day.

Meanwhile, General Meade looked at a map of Pennsylvania and saw a tiny village called Gettysburg. The Union commander had never heard of it, but he marched his tired men there on narrow, dusty country roads over meadows and through forests, believing Lee and his troops were somewhere in the area. The huge 100,000-man Army of the Potomac, one of the largest in the war, practically blotted out the horizon as it rambled toward the little village of Gettysburg, all the men and all the horses forming one giant horde. People who watched it go by were startled at its size.

Lee had a problem. Meade's army was huge, and it was all in one place. Lee's was not. Parts of his force were riding and marching miles apart. He had at first intended to attack Harrisburg and its train lines, but now he feared Meade's massive army could attack and defeat him. So he ordered his scattered forces to slow down in some places and speed up in others so that within a few days they would be together again.

At a meeting with General Isaac Trimble in late June, Lee was surprised to hear that Trimble considered the army stronger than ever.

General Robert E. Lee
That is, I hear, the general impression.

As both men rose to leave, Lee stared down at the map of the area and pointed to the small village of Gettysburg, a place he was hearing more and more rumors about.

General Robert E. Lee
Tomorrow, Gentlemen, we shall not move to Harrisburg as we expected, but go over to Gettysburg and see what General Meade is after. . . . Hereabout, we shall probably meet the army and fight a great battle, and if God gives us the victory the war will be over and we shall achieve the recognition of our independence.

Surrounding the sleepy town of Gettysburg were miles of beautiful rolling hills and productive farmland.

General John Gordon, Confederate Army
The valley [Gettysburg] awakened the most conflicting emotions. It was a delight to look upon such a scene of universal thrift and plenty. Its broad grain fields, clad in golden garb, were waving their welcome to the reapers and binders. Some fields were already dotted with harvested shocks. The huge barns on the highest ground meant to my sore-footed marchers a mount, a ride and a rest on broad-backed horses. On every side, as far as our alert vision could reach, all aspects and conditions conspired to make this fertile and carefully tilled region a panorama both interesting and enchanting. It was an eye of the fair and fertile valley of at its best, before it became the highway of armies and the ravages of war had left it wasted and bare.

This melancholy contrast between these charming districts, so similar in other respects, brought to our Southern sensibilities a touch of sadness.

In both these lovely valleys were the big red barns. . . . In both were the old-fashioned brick or stone mansions. . . . In both were the broad green meadows with luxuriant grasses and crystal springs.

The evening of June 30, Union General John Buford told the other Union officers that a massive Confederate strike would probably come the next morning, July 1. He said the Confederates were going to be to the right of them, tens of thousands of them, and that the main Union force was still some miles away.

General John Buford
They will attack you in the morning and they will come booming—skirmishers three deep. You will have to fight like the devil until supports arrive.

General Meade, a few miles away, received the message from Buford after he had been in charge of the Army of the Potomac for two days. Meade moved slowly and carefully. He had parts of his army in different places around Gettysburg.

Meade aide
He did not have time to give the subject as much reflection as he ought to give it, having been so pressed with the duties incident upon taking command.

Then Meade received another note from Buford.

General John Buford
We need help now.

Meade then sent out a second set of orders in which he wisely told all his officers not to dispatch men in different directions, but to hold the army together as it was and move it—together as one—to Gettysburg.

Around that time, Confederate General James Pettigrew led several thousand of his men toward Gettysburg. His scouts told him that Buford and his cavalry were already there. Previously, General Lee had told all his generals that he still had too many men in too many places and was trying to get them all together for an attack on Union forces in and around Gettysburg. He did not want them separated by miles. So he ordered Pettigrew and others to return to Lee's main camp at Cashtown and not engage the Union troops if they found them earlier. Pettigrew did that, bringing all his men to Cashtown and not firing a single shot.

What Lee did not know was that a massive Union Army was just about on his doorstep.

The Union Army settled in for an overnight camp next to Union Mills where, ironically, Stuart and his men had camped the previous night.

William Shriver was the manager of the mill. That night, his sister stayed over at this house and was startled by what she saw out her window as night fell—a mammoth field of fires and Union soldiers.

S. C. Shriver, letter to her sister

Campfires are burning all over the hills. Every now and then we hear the report of a gun which our Provost Guard tells me is the men killing cattle of which there is an immense drove. I know our dear Lord will protect us, and our Blessed Mother will watch over us.

PART TWO

July 1–Day One of the Battle of Gettysburg

There had been some fighting in the early morning of July 1, but it was not until the middle of the afternoon that both armies started to arrive in the village of Gettysburg and lay claim to different neighborhoods—although both armies also hurried to make it through the town as swiftly as possible and join their commanders.

Those commanders rode about the village and surrounding fields trying to gather up their men and arms and put them in position for the fight they knew was coming. Their actions drew praise from some soldiers and criticism—heavy criticism—from others. One Union soldier was very critical of General Howard's advance by his right flank and thought it was foolish.

Union soldier

It was an act of unspeakable folly. Instead of advancing, we should have fallen back as soon as the approach of the enemy from the right was developed, and should have . . . barricaded the line with our right well upon the town, and our left connecting, as well as might be, with the right of the first Corps. We could then have punished the enemy more severely and perhaps have held the town until dark. I do not know who is responsible for the advance, but whoever ordered it deserves the severest censure.

Another Union soldier, from Illinois, took a very different view.

Union lieutenant, Illinois

The enemy advanced slowly and carefully. Our first position proved to be well taken. Scattering my men to the right and to the left at intervals of 30 feet and behind posts and rail fences . . . I directed them to throw their carbine sights up for 800 yards and gave the enemy the benefits of long-range practice. . . . The firing was rapid from our carbines and induced the belief of four times the number actually present.

Gettysburg was nothing more than a quiet little village, connected to nearby towns by narrow dirt roads used by farmers. It could get quite cold in the winter and oppressively hot in the summer. Its population had always hovered around 2,400—sometimes a few hundred more and sometimes a few hundred less.

The largest business in the town was a small shoe factory (many mistakenly assumed Lee was running low on shoes and wanted to take the factory). All the other businesses were small and of use to farmers and practically nobody else. One Gettysburg resident described how ragtag and undersupplied the Southerners were.

Michael Jacobs, professor of mathematics and chemistry, Pennsylvania College

General [Jubal] Early, who accompanied this brigade . . . demanded of the authorities of our borough 1,200 pounds of sugar, 600 pounds of coffee, 60 barrels of flour, 1,000 pounds of salt, 7,000 pounds of bacon, 10 barrels of whiskey, ten barrels of onions, 1,000 pairs of shoes, and 500 hats, amounting in value to $6,000 or so; in lieu thereof, $5,000 in cash. To this demand Messrs Kendlehart and A. D. Buehler, as representatives of the town council, replied in substance that it was impossible to comply with their demands and that the goods were not in town or within reach, *that the borough had no funds and that the council had no authority to borrow either in the name of the borough or county, and that, as we were at the mercy of the General and his men, they could search and take from citizens and the empty stores whatsoever they might be able to find. No attempt was made to force the requisition and but few of the houses . . . were robbed.*

The woods that surrounded the Gettysburg area were full of white oak trees, sycamore, hickory, black walnut, chestnut, and elm. Around the forests, brooks, and ample clusters of stone were wide, vast farmlands, mostly owned by local inhabitants. From time to time a house or an old barn could be seen. Stray animals wandered around nearby fields and men with plows got up early in the morning for their daily chores, often with their sons alongside to help them. All the farmers and their sons dreaded working in the fields in early July. It was the hottest time of the year in southern Pennsylvania.

Nearby were wide valleys and small mountain chains that later connected to larger ones. South Mountain, part of a chain, was near Gettysburg, and two major roadways cut through it. One was an east-west route that ran from Philadelphia to the Cashtown Gap. The other cut through South Mountain and ended southward near Harpers Ferry. In late June of 1863, the sides of these roads were lined with tiny campfires at night—a landbound constellation of fires to match the fire in the sky from millions of bright stars—and from time to time small white canvas tent cities could be seen along the roadways. They all moved, too, as the men and horses in them moved—all moving toward something up ahead near the town of Gettysburg.

At about this time on that first day of July, another Southern general, General James Pettigrew, approached Gettysburg from the west, missing the chance to hook up with Lee's army. General John Buford, head of Meade's Union cavalry, was in the Gettysburg area and learned that Confederate troops had been there and just left. He prepared to chase the Confederates but learned that Confederate General Ambrose

Hill's entire division of troops had reached the Cashtown area and had started marching to Gettysburg. Southern General Richard Ewell's corps, also nearby, started a march that took them into Gettysburg as well. Buford, the Union cavalry commander, found himself next door to Gettysburg and decided to take his men into the village, which was getting very crowded.

For odd reasons that no one could explain, men on both sides had been pulled toward Gettysburg and generals on both sides realized that a great battle, a battle that might end the war, might be fought there. No one wanted that, but it was getting to be a possibility—a probability.

Nobody who lived in the village thought either army would come to their home, and, more important, certainly did not believe that two very large armies would engage in a bloody and protracted battle there. The residents were hoping that there would be no battle at all, and, if there was, it would take place several miles away.

The governor of Pennsylvania, a target of the South and a man caught in the middle of it all, did nothing and thought it was enough to let the Union Army protect his state. Ironically, nailed to several trees in the Gettysburg area were signs that warned people that anyone firing a gun would be fined.

Tillie Pierce, a fifteen-year-old resident of Gettysburg, her head spinning from so many uniforms right in her neighborhood, described their arrival well. Pierce was a student in a class at the Theological Seminary.

Tillie Pierce

Rushing to the door and standing on the front portico, we beheld in the direction of the Theological Seminary a dark, dense mass moving toward town. Our teacher, Mrs. Eyster, at once said, "Children, run home as quickly as you can." It did not require repeating. I am positive some of the girls did not reach their homes before the rebels were in the streets. As for myself, I had scarcely reached the front door when, on looking up the street, I saw some of the men on horseback. I scrambled in, slammed shut the door and hastened to the sitting room, peeped out between the shutters. What a horrible sight. . . . There they were, riding wildly pell-mell down the hill toward our home, shouting, yelling most unearthly, cursing, brandishing their revolvers and firing right and left. I was fully persuaded that the rebels had actually come at last. What they would do with us was a fearful question to my young mind.

A short time later, to the surprise of all, General Buford, unaware that there were Rebels in the small town, arrived with his entire force.

....

Tillie Pierce

Buford's men passed northwardly along Washington Street, headed towards Chambersburg Street, and passed out in the direction of the Theological Seminary. It was to me a novel and grand sight. I had never seen so many soldiers at one time. . . . I then knew we had protection and that they were our dearest friends.

A small crowd of "us girls" were standing on the corner of Washington and High streets as these soldiers passed by. Desiring to encourage them, who, as we were told, would before long be in battle, my sister started to sing the old war song "Our Union Forever." As some of us did not know the whole [song], we kept repeating the chorus.

Thus, we sought to cheer our brave men, and we felt amply repaid when we saw that our efforts were appreciated. Their countenances brightened and we received their thanks and cheers.

Both armies were playing a massive game of hide-and-seek in and around Gettysburg. A boy with a spyglass saw the troops of Confederate General Ambrose Hill massing to attack. He heard a roar downstairs and looked down to see the arriving troops of Union General Buford.

John Buford knew that Union general John Reynolds was on his way, determined to move his men into proper defensive formations in and around the town. Buford wanted to send a message to Reynolds, because

Buford and his men were nearly surrounded by Rebels already and in trouble. To do so, Buford climbed to the cupola on top of the seminary. It was an open-sided, square structure that gave Buford good visibility to send messages. The only problem was that he had to keep climbing up to the cupola, a target for the enemy, to send each message. A Union soldier asked him why he thought it was so important to reach Reynolds. Buford pointed out to the countryside, to a large group of Confederates who might ambush Reynolds if he had no warning. The soldier nodded.

The messages did much good in the short run. Reynolds ultimately found Buford in town and discussed the looming fight with him. Reynolds then rode off to advise other Union officers in and around Gettysburg. But he was not gone long when he was shot in the neck and killed by a Confederate. Reynolds, one of the most beloved commanders in the US Army, died right there.

Following General Reynolds's death, the Northerners and Southerners fought intensely at the seminary. Lee's army moved quickly toward the village. So did Meade's.

Tillie Pierce made it back home ahead of the fighting—in time to cross paths with the Rebels again.

Tillie Pierce

Just previous to the raid, the citizens had sent their horses out on the Baltimore Pike as far as the cemetery. There they were to be kept until those having the care of them were signaled the enemy was about, and they were to hasten as far as possible in the direction of Baltimore. Along with this party, father sent our own horse in the charge of the hired boy we then had living with us. . . . I was very much attached to the animal, for she was gentle and very pretty. I had often ridden her.

The Confederate cavalry came so suddenly that no signal was given. As they were passing our house my mother beckoned to the raiders and several rode over to where she was standing and asked what was the matter. Mother said to them, "You don't want the boy?"

One of the men replied, "No, we don't want the boy You can have him. We are only after the horses."

After we saw that the boy was safe, mother and I began to plead for the horse. As I stood there begging and weeping . . . one impudent and coarse Confederate said to me, "Sissy, What are you crying about. Go into the house and mind your business." I felt so indignant about his treatment [that] I'd have had some manner of revenge on the fellow.

The Union forces got to Gettysburg first and took Seminary Ridge, a slope next door to a Lutheran seminary. It was a long east-west slope that offered any army on top of it excellent field position to fire down upon an enemy. When Lee's men arrived, they were forced to take the bottom of the ridge and fire upward—far more difficult than firing down.

Teenager Amelia Harmon and her aunt lived west of Seminary Ridge, placing them directly in the path of the advancing Confederate forces.

Amelia Harmon

We had decided to remain in the house . . . although most of our neighbors had abandoned their houses, for ours was of the old-fashioned fortress type with 18-inch walls and very heavy shutters. My aunt and I . . . were quite alone, our farmer having gone away with the horses in hopes of hiding them in the vastness of the hills.

There were two loud blasts of cannon fire. We rushed to the windows.

All of General Lee's men and cannon were organized there at the bottom of Seminary Ridge. Lee did not know how to attack the Union troops at the top of the hill, and General Meade, up at the top (who by now had been in command of the Army of the Potomac for a whole three days), was not certain what he should do with Lee at the bottom.

Neither Lee nor Meade ever wanted, ever expected to meet at this time in this tiny farm town. But the soldiers, for their part, were ready to go.

J. F. J. Caldwell, an officer under Confederate General Ambrose P. Hill, stated the philosophy of the Confederate Army plainly just before the clash at Gettysburg.

Lieutenant J. F. J. Caldwell, Confederate Army

[Our own] numbers were not imposing, for the force of infantry did not exceed 60,000. But we were veterans, thoroughly experienced in all that relates to the march or the battlefield, sufficiently drilled to perform any maneuver at all likely to be demanded, sufficiently disciplined to obey all orders promptly and with energy, yet preserving enough of the proud individuality of Southern men to feel the cause our own, and therefore to be willing to encounter the greatest amount of personal danger and moral responsibility. The world probably never saw all the advantages of the volunteer and the regular systems so admirably combined.

In addition to this, we were in excellent health, and more properly equipped than at any period prior. . . . It is undoubtedly the moral force which enables a man to engage or to endure peril, but it is equally true that the physical condition has an incalculable influence on the spiritual system.

A last and vastly important element in the army was the confidence of the troops in the valor of their comrades and the skill of their officers. . . . The victories of 1862 and the great Battle of Chancellorsville this year had led us to believe anything scarcely impossible to Lee's army and the management of our Generals, which had wrung even from the North the highest encomiums, gave us assurance that every particle of our strength and courage would be most judiciously and powerfully applied. Lee, in himself, was a tower of strength. . . . He had ruined every Northern general sent against him, not merely with the South . . .

[but] in the eyes of their own people [Northerners]. . . . He now appeared to be invincible, immovable.

Northern soldiers were just as proud of their army, and just as ready to go.

Captain Samuel Fiske, Union Army

Our troops are making tremendous marches . . . and, if the enemy is anywhere, we shall be likely to find him . . . pretty soon. For sixteen days we have been on the move and feel the fatigues of the march well. There is much less struggling and much less pillaging than in any march of the troops that I have yet accompanied. Our men are now veterans and acquainted with the ways and resources of campaigning. There are very few sick among us. The efficient strength, in proportion to our numbers, is vastly greater than when we were given volunteers. So the Potomac Army, reduced greatly in numbers, as it has been by the expiration of the term of service of so many regiments, is still a numerous and formidable army.

Yet, Fiske felt wistful as they marched through the beautiful countryside, knowing what was to come.

Captain Samuel Fiske

Our marches . . . have been through the loveliest country across the state of Maryland to the east of Frederick City. . . . It is a cruel thing to roll the terrible wave of war over such a scene of peace, plenty, and fruitfulness, but it may be that here on our own soil and in these latest sacrifices and efforts, the great struggle for the salvation of our country and Union may successfully terminate. Poor old Virginia is so bare and desolate as to be only fit for a battleground, but it seems as if we must take our turn, too, in the Northern states, of invasion, and learn something of the practical meaning of war in our own peaceful communities.

Just before Lee decided to attack the Union Army at Gettysburg—which he did not want to do from that position—Meade tried to reorganize his troops—which he did not want to do just yet. On June 29, Meade complained that he was trying to find and defeat Lee with no intelligence, and with an army he had just taken command of.

General Alfred Pleasonton, Union Cavalry commander

General Meade, in strong terms, deprecated the change in commanders with a battle so near at hand, acknowledged his ignorance with regard to the army in general, and said he would be obliged to depend a great deal on me to assist him. . . . Our relations were of the most cordial and friendly character. . . . While the General and myself were in conversation in relation to the campaign . . . a dispatch was brought to him stating that Stuart and his cavalry were making a raid near Washington [actually Sykesville, Maryland, thirty miles north of Washington] and had cut the wires, so that we had no telegraphic communication. I laughed at this news and said that Stuart had served us better than he is aware of. We shall now have no instruction from the [War Department] until we have a battle.

This fight that Lee and Meade did not want at this time and this place, the Battle of Gettysburg, with nearly 200,000 troops in total but no real plan for either side, began with the death of Union General Reynolds on its first day and ended after two more days as the single bloodiest fight of the entire war.

On the morning of July 1, General Longstreet met with his commander, General Lee, and again pleaded for a retreat from the village. Longstreet did not want to fight at Gettysburg, not at all, and again told Lee this. Both believed their chances might be better somewhere else, even though the divisions and cavalry on both sides were quickly falling into place.

Lee, tired of Longstreet's never-ending complaints about the Gettysburg battlefield, stared at him long and hard.

General Robert E. Lee
If the enemy is there, then we must attack him.

It disturbed Lee that on several occasions his No. 2 man publicly disagreed with his plans. After the war, criticism of Longstreet at Gettysburg was severe.

Confederate officer
General Lee died believing that he lost Gettysburg by Longstreet's . . . disobedience to orders.

Critics of Longstreet were outweighed by his supporters, though.

Editor, *Houston Chronicle*
If any man or woman doubts or calls into question the record of James Longstreet as a soldier, let him or her ask the veteran southern soldier who followed him . . . what they think of him and with one voice they will say, "He was Lee's warhorse." When we heard Longstreet was in the lead or in command, or was coming, we knew that victory would follow the fighting; we trusted him. Lee trusted him. The army trusted him.

In later years, many others agreed with him.

Editor, *Atlanta Constitution*
Hereafter, truth will take hold upon the pen of history and rewrite much that has been miswritten of this great son of the South.

William Garrett Piston, historian
While [Longstreet's] account of the battle [of Gettysburg] was not without errors, it was essentially accurate. Indeed, his writings might have won considerable approval if he had taken into account, when composing them, that Lee had become a saint.

That morning, Lee did not know where Meade was, but announced to his generals:

General Robert E. Lee
Meade is marching this way.

No one else had reported on Meade's position at that time. Did Lee make it up? Did he have an incredible sense about Meade's thoughts and plans?

General Lee did not know what was happening around him in the Gettysburg area. The headstrong General Stuart had suddenly taken off with his troops and Lee had no idea where his cavalry officer was. Stuart had promised to keep in touch with Lee but had not. Lee was extremely angry. Stuart might have provided much vital information, but actually provided very little.

Attacking the Union force had been Lee's plan from the first hour that he led his men out of Virginia. Lee, more than any other Southern general, was certain that a sudden invasion of the North would be a military victory—and a public relations victory, too. It would have scared Northern politicians, and Northern citizens, begging for a settlement and lead to a Southern victory. It all might be accomplished in a few weeks. It had to start here, at tiny Gettysburg, though. This is where they were. This is where they would fight.

Meade believed the same thing. A victory here, the destruction of fabled General Lee's army, would crush the South and bring victory—right here, right now.

Both knew for sure that a lot of men would be severely wounded, and a lot of men would die. Would it be a heroic fight? Likely. Would it determine the course of the Civil War? Probably. Who would win? At this point, both Lee and Meade believed they would.

The sprawling farmland of Gettysburg that looked so serene a few days ago would be drenched in blood from both sides. It would quickly become an open-air hospital. What would happen there would be discussed in big cities and small villages for the rest of American history.

Seminary Ridge and Cemetery Hill

And so, with the Union in command of the huge Seminary Ridge and Cemetery Hill, lined up in the form of a fishhook, and the South and its cannons arrayed across more than a mile to the south of them, the Battle of Gettysburg began with bursts of cannon fire and the constant movement of troops.

The positioning of the troops was odd, with one side, the Union, in a superior position, but the other side, the South, a force led by a quick-witted, flexible, and highly creative commander, Lee.

Union General Herman Haupt, an engineer on the scene in Gettysburg, sent a telegram to General Henry Halleck in Washington informing him that Lee was there in Gettysburg, not at Chambersburg, as had been believed.

....

General Herman Haupt
The movement on their [the Confederates] part is very hurried. Meade should, by all means, be informed and be prepared for a sudden attack from Lee's whole army.

Lee had expected all of Longstreet's men to be ready for battle early that morning, and was surprised when he rode to their position and saw that no one was there. No one. He was angry. Longstreet had joined Stuart among the missing, and both were gone at the exact moment the battle seemed to be starting.

Unable to find Longstreet that day, Lee did find General John Bell Hood.

General Robert E. Lee, to Hood

The enemy is here and if we do not whip him, he will whip us.

After Lee left, Longstreet rode up to Hood.

General James Longstreet, to Hood

The General [Lee] is a little nervous this morning; he wishes me to attack. I do not wish to do so without Pickett. I never like to go into battle with one boot off.

◆

The several hundred cannon on both sides became a vibrant and lethal part of the battle on that first day at Gettysburg, Some soldiers said they had never seen cannon used so brilliantly in any battle. One artillery cannoneer in General Meade's army explained their use in a postwar essay.

Private Augustus Buell, Union Army

How those peerless cannoneers sprang to their work. . . . The very guns became things of life—not implements, but comrades. Every man was doing the work or two or three. At our gun at the finish there were only the Corporal, No. 1, and No. 3, with two drivers fetching ammunition. The water in Pat's bucket was like ink. His face and hands were smeared all over with burnt powder. The thumbstall of No. 3 was burned to a crisp by the hot vent field. Between the black of the burnt powder and the crimson streaks from his bloody head, Packard looked like a demon from below!

Up and down the line men reeling and falling, splinters flying from wheels and axles where bullets hit; in the rear, horses tearing and plunging, mad with wounds of terror; drivers yelling, shells bursting, shock shrieking overhead, howling about our ears, throwing up great clouds of dust where they struck, the musketry crashing on three sides of us, bullets hissing, humming and whistling everywhere, cannon roaring, all crash on crash and peal on pealed.

Smoke, dust, splinters, blood, wreck and carnage indescribable, but the brass guns of old B still bellowed and not a man or boy flinched or faltered. Every man's shirt soaked with sweat and many of them sopped with blood from wounds not severe enough to make such bull dogs "let go"—bare headed, sleeves rolled up, faces blackened—oh! If such a picture could be spread on canvas to life! Out in front of us an undulating field, filled almost as far as the eye could reach with a long, low, gray line creeping toward us, fairly fringed with flame.

While all that was going on, Confederates under General Ewell changed direction on their march to meet Lee at Cashtown and headed for Gettysburg. Union General Oliver Howard, hearing reports on fighting in Gettysburg, headed there as well. By about 2:00 P.M. Howard's army had joined the Union troops outside the town and Ewell joined the Confederate forces. Cannons fired regularly. At about 2:30 P.M. all the armies, North and South, were in place in the fishhook pattern and the Battle of Gettysburg was underway.

The Confederates did not do well on that first day of battle. They were defeated in fights large and small, starting in the early morning. Lee had not planned the first day of attacks well, and he and his men were surprised that they were not being fired upon directly going up the hills, where they had little defense. Instead, the fire came from their sides, as a young Confederate soldier, Lieutenant Randolph McKim, explained later in his diary.

CULP'S HILL

Lieutenant Randolph McKim, Confederate Army

Then came General Ewell's order to assume the offensive and assault the crest of Culp's Hill, on our right. . . . The works to be stormed ran at almost right angles to those we occupied. Moreover, there was a double line of entrenchments, one above the other, and each filled with troops. In moving to the attack we were exposed to enfilading fire from the wood on our left flank, besides the double line of fire which we had to face in front, and a battery of artillery posted on a hill to our left rear opened upon us at short distance.

Culp's Hill, owned at the time by a local man, Henry Culp, that from the side resembled a mammoth earthen "saddle," with troops all over it, was vital. It was part of the overall land defense of the entire Gettysburg plan, provided a jumping-off point for any attack on Cemetery Hill and protected the Baltimore Pike, the road on which supplies were taken. Occupation of it was crucial to both sides.

The Union Army used its oldest commander, General George S. Greene, to occupy it with the XII Corps. Greene built a large, strong series of breastworks, long deep ditches for defense of the ground, that proved very effective. The Confederates attacked it, unsuccessfully, on the afternoon of day two. Lee ordered it assaulted again on the morning of day three, but they were turned back after three attacks around 10:00 A.M. and Culp's Hill remained in Union possession.

Randolph McKim's diary continued

In the meantime, on swept the gallant little brigade, the Third North Carolina, to the right of the line, next the Second Maryland, then the three Virginia regiments (10th, 23rd, and 37th) with the first North Carolina on the extreme left. Its ranks had been sadly thinned, and its energies greatly depleted by those six fearful hours of battle that morning, but its nerves and spirit were undiminished. Soon, however, the left and center were checked and then repulsed, probably by the severe flank fire from the woods, and the small remnant of the Third North Carolina with the stronger Second Maryland (I do not recall the banners of any other regiment) were far in advance of the rest of the line. On they pressed to within twenty or thirty paces of the breastworks—a small but gallant band of heroes daring to attempt what could not be done by the flesh and blood. The (Confederates) were not successful in pushing the Northerners back.

The end soon came. The Confederates were beaten back to the line from which we had advanced with terrible loss, and in much confusion, but the enemy did not make a countercharge. By the strenuous efforts by the officers of the line, and of the staff, order was restored and we re-formed in the breastworks from which we had emerged, there again to be exposed to an artillery fire exceeding in violence that of the early morning. . . .

It remains only to say that . . . this single brigade was hurled unsupported against the enemy works. . . . [General Junius] Daniel's brigade remained in the breastworks during and after the charge, and neither from that command nor from any other had we any support. Of course it is to be presumed that General Daniel acted in obedience to orders. We remained in this breastwork after the charge about an hour before we finally abandoned the Federal entrenchment and retired to the front of the hill.

The Union army had a number of gallant officers, middle-rank officers, who did not get as much public notice as the major players, such as Meade. One was Brigadier General Francis Barlow, of the 61st New York Volunteer Infantry Regiment, whose presence and hard work on the battlefield went almost unnoticed by officers and newsmen.

Captain Charles Francis Adams, Union Army

I am more disposed to regard Barlow as a military genius than any man I have yet seen.

And then there were men seen as geniuses and heroes who were not, or whose heroism was overrated. Such was the case with the Southern attack on Cemetery Hill that appeared to give the Confederates victory. It was a wild and colorful attack, accompanied by loud waves of Confederate yelling.

General Robert E. Lee

[The Yankees] were entirely routed.

But they were not. The "routed" Yankees held their own and held on until reinforcements arrived—and then they set up a new and stronger line. In fact, many military observers later noted that if the Confederates had pressed harder on Cemetery Hill that first day, they might have won both it and the overall battle. But they did not.

Lee's view was that if they could not win on day one, they would surely win on day two. He was not worried.

An ongoing problem was the confusion between Cemetery Hill and Seminary Ridge. Union General Howard constantly talked about and planned to occupy "Cemetery Hill," unaware that the hill in question was Seminary Ridge.

Major Charles Wainwright, 1st New York Artillery

Howard wanted Cemetery Hill to be held at all costs.

Aide to Major Charles Wainwright

[Someone] came to us and asked [us to] hold Cemetery Hill. Not knowing there was a cemetery on the hill, I thought it was Seminary Hill [there was a seminary on that hill].

Wainwright and his men remained on Cemetery Hill, by mistake, most of the afternoon.

Sensing a large assault on the morning of July 1 from the Cashtown area, where General Lee had his headquarters, Union general Buford, in command of only his cavalry, decided to attempt to stop the Confederates, or at least hold their assault, until Federal infantry could join him. It was a risky decision. To do so, he set up his defenses in three areas of high ground—Herr Ridge, Seminary Ridge, and McPherson Ridge—all just west of Gettysburg. If the Rebels held spots around the town heights, it would be difficult for Meade's men, no matter how large their number, to dislodge the Confederates from those positions, and would put the Union at a distinct disadvantage.

Two brigades under Confederate general Henry Heth were the first to meet Union troops around Gettysburg as they marched on the Chambersburg Pike. A small force of Buford's cavalry fired upon Heth's men, stopping them for the time being. Legend has it that the first shot of that engagement was fired by Union lieutenant Marcellus Jones of the 8th Illinois Cavalry. That was around 7:30 A.M. The Confederates had superior numbers, but Buford's men held them up for nearly three hours, firing from behind fences and trees. The Southerners eventually pushed Buford's men back to McPherson Ridge, where they were joined by the first wave of General John Reynolds's men. (Reynolds would be killed shortly after he arrived.)

The Confederates were defeating the North on the Chambersburg Pike until the Federals were reinforced by the many more Union troops around a railroad cut. South of the cut, General James Archer's Confederate soldiers joined the fight, aided by Heth's entire force, assisted by the entire number of troops under Confederate General James Pettigrew. Heth's men successfully engaged Union troops but were pushed back by the arrival of the already famed Iron Brigade—a unit of the Army of the Potomac comprised of men from Indiana, Michigan, and Wisconsin and led by General John Gibbon. The Iron Brigade halted the Confederates and captured several hundred men, including General Archer himself.

Union colonel Abner Doubleday took over command of Reynolds's army upon his death and fought on until shortly after noon on that first day.

At about 2:30 P.M., the Federals were smashed with the arrival of Heth's force, Pettigrew's men, and others. The fighting was intense. In the 26th North Carolina, only 212 of the 839 men survived the carnage. General Early's men arrived and helped push the Federals back. Union positions weakened and they departed north and west of town and sought refuge at the top of Cemetery Hill.

Upon learning of Reynolds's death, Meade sent Major General Winfield Scott Hancock into the field with instructions to head up that army and to determine whether the area around Gettysburg, and Gettysburg itself, was the right place for a mass confrontation with Lee. Hancock looked around and talked it over with a few other officers.

General Winfield Scott Hancock, to General Oliver Otis Howard
I think this is the strongest position by nature upon which to fight a battle that I ever saw.

Howard agreed.

General Winfield Scott Hancock
Very well, sir, I select this as the battlefield.

General Lee sent orders to General Early to take Cemetery Hill, where the Federals were quickly trying to give themselves a strong defensive position. But Lee's order to Early ended with a phrase that caused great confusion and has resounded through history.

General Robert E. Lee
[Take the hill]. . . . If practicable . . .

Lee should have simply ordered Early to take the hill, no matter what. Early misunderstood the order. He did not think it was "practicable" and never tried to take Cemetery Hill. The Federals continued to gather there until they were at full strength. It was a big mistake on Early's part not to attack the hill, and a larger mistake on Lee's part to send him such a tentative order.

If Early had taken Cemetery Hill and chased the Federals from it, the South, holding that position, might have won the battle. They would have remained at full strength, too, because there might not have been a Pickett's Charge. The Southerners could have marched on to Harrisburg, seized the trains, and gone into Philadelphia and/or New York. If Lee had looked into a crystal ball, it might have shown a victory for the South in the Civil War. But none of that was "practicable."

The Union held Cemetery Hill all day and through the night.

The Fighting in Town

On the first day of the battle, townspeople in Gettysburg realized they were going to be caught up in the fight. The Federals had fled from the Harmon house as the Confederates advanced into the town. Amelia Harmon and her aunt hid in the basement of the house, afraid to run outside into a hail of bullets from both sides.

Amelia Harmon

A swish like the mowing of grass on the front lawn, then a dense shadow darkened the low, grated cellar windows. It is the sound and shadow of hundreds of marching feet. We can see them to the knees only but the uniforms are the Confederate gray! Now we understand the scurrying of feet overhead. Our soldiers . . . have been driven back . . . have left the house and have left us to our fate.

We rushed up the cellar steps to the kitchen. The barn was in flames and cast a lurid glare through the window. The house was filled with rebels and they were deliberately firing it. They had taken down a file of newspaper for kindling, piled on books, rags, and furniture and applied matches to ignite the pile . . . already a tiny flame was curling upward. We both jumped on the fire in hopes of extinguishing it, and pleaded with them in pity to spare our home. But there was no pity in those determined faces. . . .

We fled from our burning house only to encounter worse horrors. The first rebel line of battle had passed our house and was now engaged in a hot skirmish in the gorge at Willoughby Run. The second line was being advanced just abreast of the barn, and at that moment was being hotly attacked by the Union troops with shot and shell! We were between the lines. To go towards town would be to walk into the jaws of death. Only one way was open—through the ranks of the whole Confederate army to safety in its rear!

Bullets whistled past our ears. Shells burst and scattered their deadly contents around us, the line moving forward as they fired. On we hurried—wounded men falling all around us, the line moving forward as they fired, it seemed, with deadly precision, past what seemed miles of artillery with horses galloping like mad towards the town. We were objects of wonder and amazement, that was certain, but few took time to listen to our story and none believed it. All kept hurrying us to the rear. "Go on! Go on!" they shouted, "Out of reach of grape and canister."

At last, after we had walked perhaps two miles, we came upon a group of officers and newspapermen in conference under a tree. We told them our story. The officers looked incredulous, the newspapermen attentive. One of these, the Confederate correspondent for the London Times, *seemed greatly interested in our tale and was, I believe, the only one who credited it fully. He courteously offered to conduct us to a place of safety further to the rear.*

The correspondent kept his word, hurrying to General Lee to tell Amelia's tale and the story of her home being set on fire. He said the two women were starving and Lee had his men give them a day's rations.

The morning fight was fierce and a mass of slowly unfolding confusion. The Rebels found Union troops where they did not expect them and the Federals were pushed back by lines of Confederate soldiers they did not know were located in places near them. It was a sign that the fight at Gettysburg, no matter how long it lasted, would be chaotic and quickly changing.

A vigorous Southern assault on the Union line in town caused it to buckle. In the fight, Colonel Doubleday was trying to repel

Southerners pouring through his line from two directions and had his hands full. All his officers and men held their positions as the best they could.

Private Augustus Buell, Union Army

We were formed . . . "straddle" of the railroad cut, the Old Man with the three guns forming the right half-battery on the north side, and Davison with the three guns of the left half on the south side. Stewart's three guns were somewhat in advance of ours, forming a slight echelon in half-battery while our three guns were in open order, bringing the left gun close to the Cashtown Road. We were formed in a small field . . . and our guns raked the road at the top of the low crest forming the east bank of Willoughby Run. . . . Hall's and Reynolds's batteries . . . which had held our front all morning, had retired into the streets of Gettysburg down onto the road near the seminary and all the infantry of the 1st Corps that had been fighting in our front had fallen back.

But Private Buell and his comrades had some luck.

Private Augustus Buell

Directly in our front . . . rebel infantry had been forced to halt and lie down by the tornado of canister that we had given them from the moment they came in over the bank of the creek.

In a few moments, the Union had a clean view of the entire Rebel line and opened fire.

Private Augustus Buell

To the northwest, Rebels attacked the federal line. Then, for seven or eight minutes, ensued probably the most desperate fight ever waged between infantry and artillery, at close range without a particle of cover.

In the late afternoon of that first day, the village of Gettysburg was in total chaos. Townspeople, fearful of an attack from either side, were running with suitcases through the streets of the town to escape or find refuge in a friend's home. They were joined by thousands of Southern soldiers, many yelling, who were trying to claim victory in the town; others were trying to get through it to attack Union forces on the other side. At the same time, Union troops, shaken by the turmoil, were running the other way. Each side claimed many confused prisoners.

Major Rufus Dawes, 6th Wisconsin

The streets were jammed with crowds of retreating soldiers, and with ambulances, artillery, and wagons. The cellars were crowded with men sound in body, but craven in spirit, who had gone there to surrender.

Meade Orders a Retreat?

On the first day of the Battle of Gettysburg, to cover himself against all eventualities, General Meade issued an order to prepare a retreat from the battlefield. The point of the order was to make sure that if the Northerners were badly routed that day, the army would be able to retreat from Gettysburg in an orderly fashion and not lose hundreds of men in a doomed attack.

Some in the Union Army did not read the order that way, though. They assumed that Meade, having seen the enemy and brand new to such a large command, had decided his army could not win and was preparing to leave Gettysburg and find safety elsewhere.

To prepare, first, Meade chose a man from each corps to draw up a list of commanders and artillery pieces, along with maps of the quickest roads out of Gettysburg. He then had a very complete and highly organized list of what he needed to bring with him on a retreat—if that was forced upon him—to quickly get out of Gettysburg.

He then asked his chief of staff, General Daniel Butterfield, to draw up an order to retreat, if need be, that would merge all his armies into one to help with expediency.

From the moment the order was issued, all was confusion.

General John Gibbon, Union Army
Great God? General Meade does not intend to leave this position!

Gibbon never thought Meade would actually order a retreat or had even planned one.

General John Gibbon

[Butterfield] said something to the effect that it was necessary to be prepared, in case it should be necessary to leave, or some remark at that time. . . .

I was firmly convinced at that time that Meade had no intentions of retreating.

But the talk about a retreat grew and was offered as testimony in March of 1864, at a Congressional committee hearing on the Battle of Gettysburg. Meade, looking back, was absolutely astounded. Also at the 1864 hearing, General Daniel Sickles charged that Meade wanted to retreat just before the second day of the Gettysburg fight. His source was Butterfield. Meade nearly went into shock.

General George Meade

I did not order a retreat.

In fact, when Meade arrived on the field at Gettysburg around 4:00 P.M., his army was moving into battle and he made no effort to stop its motion. Meade used this fact to pose a thorny question at the hearing.

General George Meade

To be sure, when the question is asked, why was not the [retreat] order issued and why did not the army retreat? The gentlemen will be puzzled for an answer because you know that from the time I arrived on the ground, around 4:00 P.M. when Lee attacked, and after the attack, all day and night, there was no difficulty at any moment in withdrawing by the Taneytown Road [and others].

But Meade did not retreat.

The argument continued until 1898, when another commission, led by Lieutenant Colonel William Fox, studied the battle.

Fox was interrupted by an urgent letter from General Alexander Webb, who was with the 107th New York Regiment at Gettysburg. He urged Fox to ignore all taken testimony and documents about the so-called retreat. Although Webb did not say so, many felt the enemies of Meade from the war were gathering to ruin his reputation.

General Alexander Webb

My dear Fox, it is well for me to state here that you cannot have peace when you bring up those [retreat] questions again for discussion, in a board constituted as is our Gettysburg Commission. I cannot sign a report giving some one person's opinion as to what General Meade intended to do on July 2d, 1863. When General Meade, a Christian gentleman, has stated under oath that the charges made against him are absolutely false, I would be condemned by every officer of the Army of the Potomac who knew General Meade if I were to sign a report stating that he issued an order for the army to leave Gettysburg.

The entire "retreat" order was subsequently removed from the 1898 report and never brought up again. Meade was cleared—finally—thirty-five years later.

Meade sometimes gave long orders and complex answers to problems, but most of the time his directions and orders were short and curt—and to the point.

General John Gibbon

[At Gettysburg, General] Pleasonton came to him to ask a question about the disposition of his cavalry. It struck me that Meade answered him very curtly. "I can give you no detailed instructions but simply want you to protect well the front and flanks of this army with your cavalry."

The generals to whom Meade assigned positions often did not follow his directions. General Daniel Sickles, as an example, was well ahead of his assigned position at Gettysburg. Meade galloped across the battlefield to inform him of his error. Sickles told Meade he had made a mistake and would now move all his men to the proper position. At that moment, Meade, on horseback, heard a loud roar of cannon in the position that Sickles was about to move to. Meade shook his head from side to side, listened to another burst of cannon fire, and turned to Sickles.

General George Meade

I wish to God you could [move], but the enemy won't let you!

Sickles always admitted that he had been out of order to move his men into that untenable position, and that it had nothing to do with General Meade's order. One of his aides, Major H. E. Tremain, backed him up.

Major H. E. Tremain, Union Army

Our Corps opened the fight. We knew where the battle would begin. I felt certain, for I told General Sickles on Wednesday night, as I had been over the ground more and had therefore better opportunities for knowing that if the enemy attacked the army at all in its present position, it would be in certain localities on the left, which I designated, and Thursday morning he examined the topography and agreed with me. It was then he pressed on General Meade the necessity for changing his lines to meet such an anticipated attack. It was in that very locality, and by the roads

I designated, that the enemy did come and hurl upon us their tremendous force. . . .

At around 7:30 P.M. on the first day, Meade received a late and disturbing message from General Hancock, who was already in Gettysburg.

General Winfield Scott Hancock
When I arrived here an hour since, I found that our troops had given up the front of Gettysburg and the town. We have now taken up a position in the cemetery which cannot well be taken; it is a position, however, easily turned. [General Henry] Slocum is now coming in on the ground and is taking position on the right, which will protect the right. But we have as yet no troops on the left, the Third Corps not having yet reported. But I suppose it is marching up. If so, Sickles's flank march will in a degree protect our left flank. In the meantime, Gibbon had best march on so as to take position on our right or our left, to our rear, as may be necessary, in some commanding position.

General Gibbon will see this dispatch. All is quiet now. I think we will be all right until night. I have sent all the trains back. When night comes, it can be told better what had best be done. I think we can retire; if not we can fight here, as the ground appears not unfavorable with good troops. I will communicate within a few moments with General Slocum and transfer command to him.

The letter convinced Meade to take immediate action. He told an officer:

General George Meade
Have General [Alpheus] Williams send further orders to [General John] Sedgwick turning him forward to Gettysburg with all speed. Tell Sedgwick I will wait at Taneytown to speak with him before I go to Gettysburg.

At that hour, many Union officers who were with Meade at Taneytown did not know they would soon be on the march.

Major James Biddle, Union Army, letter to his wife

[Our troops] have come plumb up to the rebel line and the 4th of July, 1863, bids fair to have new memories associated with it. I trust equally well of hereafter honoring, as those for which we now celebrate the day.

General Meade was to work very hard and in fact we all have had hard work. I do not think we shall leave here [Taneytown], but in all probability the battle will take place here.

When Meade arrived at Taneytown, he learned that the body of the slain General Reynolds was on its way there. He told his staff officers:

General George Meade

They will pause here for you to pay your respects.

By nightfall of July 1, Meade had decided that he would engage Lee in one big battle and that it would be at Gettysburg. There would be no more talk of a fight somewhere else.

General George Meade

It seems to me we are so concentrated that a battle at Gettysburg is now forced on us and that, if we get all our people and attack with our whole force tomorrow, we ought to defeat the force the enemy has.

Shortly afterward, all of Meade's men began to march toward the tiny village in southern Pennsylvania. Meade understood that speed was of the essence now in gathering his army. He had provoked General Sickles into a furor with a terse note criticizing the slow speed of him and his troops that day.

General George Meade

The Commanding General noticed with regret the very slow movement of your corps yesterday. It is presumed that you marched at an early hour, and up to 6:00 P.M. the rear of your column had not passed Middleburg, distant from your camp of the night before of some twelve miles only. This, considering the good condition of road and the favorable state of weather, was far from meeting the expectation of the Commanding General and delayed to a very late hour the arrival of troops and trains in your rear. The Second Corps, in the same space of time, made a march nearly double your own. Situated as this army is, the Commanding General looks for rapid movement of the troops.

Meade then sent a message to General Henry Halleck, commander of all the Union armies, in Washington.

General George Meade

The First and 11th Corps have been engaged all day in front of Gettysburg. The 12th, 3rd, and 5th have been moving up and are, I hope, by this time on the field. This leaves only the 6th, which will move up tonight. General Reynolds was killed this morning, early in the action. I immediately sent up General [Winfield Scott] Hancock to assume command. [Confederate Generals] A. P. Hill and Ewell are certainly concentrating. Longstreet's whereabouts I do not know. If he is not up tomorrow, I hope, with a force I have concentrated, to defeat Hill and Ewell. . . . At any rate, I see no course other than to hazard a general battle. Circumstances during the night may alter this decision, of which I will try to advise you.

On day one of the Battle of Gettysburg, approximately 50,000 troops were engaged in the fighting, making that day, by itself, one of the twenty-five biggest battles of the war. Much more was to come.

PART THREE

July 2–Day Two of the Battle of Gettysburg

During the night of July 1, most of the armies on both sides arrived or started to arrive at Gettysburg, bringing the total troop strength on both sides to—on paper—nearly 200,000. Some thirteen or fourteen thousand more Union troops, and all their generals, arrived at Gettysburg. Confederate General George Pickett and his men (who would become so famous, or infamous, on day three of the fight) were on their way—not only more troops, but "fresh troops," in Lee's mind.

The next morning, July 2, the battle lines of both armies had been arranged in a fishhook pattern. The Union defensive lines ran from Culp's Hill, south of the village, northwest to Cemetery Hill, and then south for two miles on top of Cemetery Ridge, halting near Little Round Top, a large hill. Most of the Union troops were on top of or defending Cemetery Ridge. The Confederate line paralleled the Union line for about a mile to the west on Seminary Ridge, ran east through Gettysburg itself, and curved southeast to a point near Culp's Hill. The Union had a positional advantage, but the Confederate line was enormous, stretching for nearly five miles.

On the morning of that second day, a young Union colonel named Huntington Jackson had an unusual and quite dramatic view of his commander, General Meade, in the distance. It was early morning and a thick mist hung over the fields.

Colonel Huntington Jackson, Union Army

Meade was on the hill, dismounted, and peering through the still uncertain light to discover the lines of the enemy. The scene was impressive, and one long to be remembered. Meade—tall, slender, and nervous, his hair and whiskers tinged with gray—he was pale and careworn. The sleepless and anxious night had left him with great black lines under his eyes. On the hill, lying by the side of the graves in the old country graveyard, were the tired soldiers, still asleep. Long black guns were pointed in the direction of the peaceful valleys, and all around were broken tombstones and artillery wheels and dead horses.

The men of the Union's 2nd Corps, who were still in Taneytown, rose at daybreak to discover that many did not have breakfast.

Captain Benjamin Thompson, 2nd Corps, Union Army

We made small fires of twigs to cook our coffee and bacon. [However,] we discovered that we were out of rations. I had lost my haversack in the hustle of the day before, and my breakfast, like that of many of my men, consisted of crackers and coffee.

Shortly after what passed for breakfast, Thompson and his still-hungry men left Taneytown with General Gibbon. Gettysburg was about twelve miles away.

General John Gibbon

We got off soon after daylight, and to facilitate the march and shorten the column, the road was left, as before, to the artillery and ambulances, the infantry marching through the grain and grass fields on each side. In this way, our Corps reached the field around six o'clock.

That same morning, the Army of the Potomac received some helpful and good news from General Halleck in Washington. Meade had informed Halleck of the dangerously dwindling supplies, and the commanding general sent explicit orders.

General Henry Halleck

It is the duty of military commanders to take possession of such military supplies as are likely to fall into the hands of the enemy, or which may be necessary for the immediate wants of our own troops in the field of actual hostilities. All horses and beef cattle in such regions should be removed or taken possession [of] and reconverted to government uses. Staff officers should send out, with sufficient escorts to seize and remove all horses deemed suitable for the cavalry, artillery, or wagon trains . . . giving receipt in which the character of the animals and the service into which each should be suited. Where not required for immediate use where taken, they should be sent to the nearest depot and turned over to the depot quartermaster and Commissary. If possible, a quartermaster and Commissary or an officer acting in those capacities should accompany every [foraging] expedition. The vicinity of any railroad in our possession should not be disturbed unless in immediate danger from approaching raids.

In other words, take the food! Officers and their men took food wherever they could find it, to the anger and dismay of local farmers.

Major General D. H. Rucker, Union Army

Soon, whole fields were occupied by artillery, cavalry, ambulances, and team animals . . . all the growing fields [of] corn, oats, wheat, and grass were being stripped by grazing horses and mules to alleviate their suffering.

On the morning of that second day, most Confederates felt optimistic.

General Stephen Ramseur, Confederate Army

We are surprised that we have met with feeble resistance thus far. We feel sure, however, we will have some stern and bloody work to do before this campaign is ended.

General Robert E. Lee

The result of this day's [July 1] operations induced the belief that, with proper concert of action, and with the increased support that the positions gained on the right would enable the artillery to render the assaulting columns, we should ultimately succeed, and it was accordingly determined to continue the attack.

Lee ordered General Longstreet to lead a huge attack against the Federals around daybreak, in the hopes of smashing them. At the same time, on the left of the battlefield, Ewell was supposed to attack Culp's Hill and Cemetery Hill in a surprise movement.

Lee's plan was not complete, because on that second morning at Gettysburg he still had no idea where the marauding, usually reliable General J. E. B. Stuart and his men were. Stuart was not providing Lee with any intelligence about the Union Army or its position. Lee was trying to win a pinball game on a board with dozens of holes missing or blocked. He was very unhappy that Stuart, wandering about the countryside, would reportedly not arrive in camp until later that evening—if at all.

That morning, Longstreet—who was there and was Lee's No. 2 man (many called him Lee's "warhorse")—suggested to Lee that he take his force, move around the Union troops facing him, and attack the Union perimeter, capturing their supply trains and, from that surprise position, cutting off the Federals' escape route. Lee said no—another questionable decision. It cemented in Longstreet's head the idea that Gettysburg was the wrong place for this mammoth battle and that it would be best for Lee's army to get out of tiny little Gettysburg and retreat.

According to General McLaws, the two men argued.

General Lafayette McLaws, Confederate Army
Longstreet was irritated and annoyed.

McLaws and his men had arrived at Gettysburg around 8:00 A.M. on the morning of July 1.

General Lafayette McLaws
The march was continued at a very early hour, and my command reached the hill overlooking Gettysburg early in the morning. Just after I arrived, General Lee sent for me.

Lee showed McLaws a map of the Gettysburg area and asked him if he could get his men to a specific spot. McLaws said he had to reconnoiter the area. Lee told him Lieutenant Colonel Samuel Johnston, from his staff, was about to do just that. McLaws went with Johnston, and while doing so joined the battle.

After the war, Longstreet was often criticized for disagreeing with Lee.

Colonel E. Porter Alexander, Confederate Army
Many an old soldier may never forgive Longstreet such a sentiment, & yet I do not believe he ever knew how it reads to a lover of Lee.

Lee thought differently than Longstreet. While he had not won much on day one of the engagement, he had not lost much either. His men had won some skirmishes and lost others, as had the Union forces. His men were exhausted, but so was the enemy. Why run? He might still prevail.

The most important thing to Lee was to win here in Gettysburg, go to Harrisburg, jump on trains there and head for Philadelphia and end the war. He wanted to stay and defeat Meade and his men. How long would that take? He did not know. No one knew.

By the second day of the battle, Southern soldiers noticed a strange mode of operation of Lee's. He would take circuitous roads and pathways on and near the battlefield. These often wound up costing the Confederates time and energy, both of which were important at Gettysburg. There were complaints, too, that Lee did not provide his generals and staff with the equipment and provisions they needed to carry out his orders.

Colonel E. Porter Alexander

Scarcely any of our generals had half of what they needed to keep a constant & close supervision on the execution of important orders. . . . An army is like a great machine, and in putting it into battle it is not enough for its commander to merely issue the necessary orders. He should have a staff ample enough to supervise the execution of each step & to promptly report any difficulty or misunderstanding. There is no telling the value of the hours which were lost by that division. . . . Of course I told the officers at the head of the column of the route my artillery had followed—which was easily seen—but there was no one with authority to vary the orders they were under & they momentarily expected the new ones for which they had sent & which were very explicit when they came after the long, long delay.

Another problem Lee seemed to have, according to his generals, was lack of specific directions that left his subordinates wondering what was in his head. At one point, he ordered an attack by three different divisions, but did not say in which order they should attack. All were in confusion.

Colonel E. Porter Alexander
I did not hear of any conference or [discussions] among our generals at this time as to the best formations and tactics in making our attacks. . . . [The Lee plan] was peculiar.

During that second day at Gettysburg, more men talked of the battlefield heroism of General Longstreet. At one point, Longstreet put his hat on his sword and waved it in their air as he led General William Barksdale's men in a fierce engagement near the Peach Orchard. It even impressed Union officers there.

Union officer
Our Generals don't do that sort of thing.

In no time, Longstreet was back near Cemetery Hill to lead the attack there.

General James Longstreet told his artillery:
Let the batteries open, order great care, and precision firing.

The artillerists, though, did not seem to know in which direction they were to fire. The Union was guilty of the same mismanagement. People were sent in the wrong direction or, when winning an encounter, pulled back.

Meade was as guilty of mismanagement as Lee was. As an example, in the battle for Culp's Hill that second day, Union general John Geary could not be found. Meade sent generals, colonels, anyone he could to find him. They finally located Geary in a bivouac east of Rock Creek. All told, about 2,500 men had walked off the battlefield to find the missing general and were not available later, when Meade needed them most. Someone, somehow, should have been leading those 2,500 soldiers as a unit. No one did.

Despite all the turmoil of day two, there was no loose talk about Lee retreating from Gettysburg. It was Lee's spirit to attack, to fight—not to withdraw. He wanted very badly to attack the enemy on day two and win the battle.

A correspondent for the *London Times*, traveling with the Confederate Army, summed up the situation on the morning of day two.

Reporter, *London Times*
A cry for immediate battle . . . swelled the gale. Timid and hesitating counsels were impatiently discarded, and . . . the mature and cautious wisdom of General Lee had no choice but to float with the current, and trust the enthusiasm of his troops to carry him triumphantly . . . over the heights.

Lee and his men still had problems, such as the still very much missing cavalry of J. E. B. Stuart.

General Ambrose P. Hill, Confederate Army
The want of cavalry had been and was again seriously felt. Prudence leads me to be content with what had been gained.

At the same time that was going on, Meade was faced with dozens of notes from and about his own staff, including this message from General Sickles.

Major H. E. Tremain, aide to Sickles
In the opinion of General Sickles, more artillery than he had should be posted in order to meet the attack that was expected.

General George Meade

Generals are [always] expecting attacks on their own fronts.

Then he paused and added:

General George Meade

If General Sickles needs more artillery in case of attack, the reserve artillery could furnish it.

◆

The looting of civilian homes continued at Gettysburg on day two. A local girl, Liberty Hollinger, said the Confederates made certain that she was not hiding any Union troops in her house and then looted it.

Liberty Hollinger

[Troops] helped themselves to anything they could find . . . forced the locks on father's storehouse, and took what they wanted and then ruined everything else.

Nellie Aughinbaugh, Liberty's neighbor

[I saw] a Union soldier shot down right in front of mother's home. . . . [Minutes later] a Confederate came along and he searched the dead man's clothes. [He] found a small picture of the dead man and apparently his wife and two little children.

Her grandfather got a blanket and rolled the dead Union soldier up in it, but a few moments later another Confederate soldier went through the pockets of the slain man inside the blanket.

At that same time, rumors flew everywhere that a Confederate Army, maybe Lee's, would attack Washington, DC, and seize all the US government buildings. President Lincoln, the press complained, was doing nothing to protect the capital or the White House.

Reporter, ***New York Times***
If Nero could fiddle while Rome was burning, it is believed he finds his counterpart in Lincoln, who cat-hauls the Army of the Potomac while the rebels are positively knocking at his own doors.

In the armies of both North and South, the bloodshed on day one at Gettysburg had caused emotions to run high. As an example, Confederate general Trimble told General Ewell he wanted a division of troops to take a hill—an ordinary request.

General Isaac Trimble
Give me a brigade, even a good regiment, and I will engage to take that hill.

General Richard Ewell
When I need advice from a junior officer, I generally ask it.

General Isaac Trimble
General Ewell, I am very sorry you do not appreciate my suggestions. You will regret it as long as you live.

Confederate soldier, 57th North Carolina

There was not an officer, not even a man, who did not expect that the war would be closed upon that hill that evening. If Stonewall [Jackson] had been there, he would not have waited for orders until the morrow.

William Seymour, Louisiana Tigers, Confederate Army

Here we all felt the loss of General Jackson most sensibly. Had he been alive, and in command when we charged through the town, I am sure that he would have given his usual order—"push on the infantry."

As much as the enthusiastic men wanted to take each hill and push on, their generals realized that they were not only exhausted, but were fighting on very hot midsummer days.

Confederate soldier, 5th Alabama

It was an excessively hot day and we were going through wheat fields & ploughed ground & over fences; it almost killed us. I was perfectly exhausted & never suffered so much from heat & fatigue in my life.

Most of the Confederates had assumed the entire battle had been won on the first day. One army band even set itself up in a little town square and played "Dixie" to commemorate the "victory." They found out the next day that were wrong.

On the night before the second day, Lee seemed very preoccupied.

General John Bell Hood, Confederate Army

[Lee was] full of hope, yet at times buried in deep thought. His coat was buttoned to the throat, sabre belt buckled around the waist, field glasses pending at his side.

One more time, Longstreet told Lee and several other generals, that the Union would have an advantage sitting on top of Cemetery Ridge and other hills there. It might be more prudent, Longstreet said, to avoid a fight at Gettysburg entirely and move the Confederate Army east, where it would sit between the Union Army and Washington, in position to move either way and fight in any direction.

General James Longstreet
All we have to do is to throw our army around their left and we shall interpose between the Federal Army and Washington.

It would also enable Lee to make the Northerners come to him and force Meade to attack him at a place where the Southerners could control the hills, ravines, and other positions—exactly the opposite of what was happening at Gettysburg. Lee said no, and Longstreet, angry, said nothing more.

Lee was confident about success on day two of Gettysburg. That night he had said so, smiling, to his officers.

General Robert E. Lee
I intend to make the Yankees dance [tomorrow].

Meade felt the same way, but his demeanor was far more somber than Lee's. General Carl Schurz saw Meade on the first night after the battle.

General Carl Schurz, Union Army
. . . his long bearded, haggard face, covered by a black military felt hat, the rim of which was turned down, looked careworn and tired, as if he had not slept the night. . . .

[Meade had] nothing in his appearance or his bearing—not a smile, not a sympathetic word addressed to those around him—that might have made the hearts of the soldiers warm up to him.

Meade's predecessors always rode with a large entourage of junior officers, but Meade gave that honor to just one aide. In addition, he had promoted some junior officers over senior men—something President Lincoln had suggested. One of those who was overlooked was Colonel Abner Doubleday, who had fought well at the beginning of the fight and was very angry at Meade.

Lieutenant Colonel William Brooke Rawle, Union Army
Meade had no confidence in Doubleday.

Meade benefitted from some events he had no control over, such as the arrival of the long-marching Sixth Corps. They arrived with every man in the corps singing "John Brown's Body" as loudly as he could. They picked up the spirits of all the Union soldiers.

Lee was not ready to fight until 11:00 A.M. that second day. Neither was Longstreet. In fact, he and his men were nowhere to be found.

General Armistead Long, Confederate Army
Lee said, what can detain Longstreet? He ought to be in position by now.

Edwin Coddington, historian
[General Long's] account was offered as evidence of Lee's impatience with the slow-moving Longstreet. Doubtless, Lee was impatient with Longstreet, but also with himself.

Years later, Helen Longstreet, the general's second wife, heartily defended her husband, citing many conversations with him about the war.

Helen Longstreet

Matters on the morning of July 2 were not awaiting Longstreet's movements. All that forenoon, everything was still in the air, depending on Lee's personal examinations and final decisions. . . . At sunrise on July 2, Lee himself did not know where to attack. He did not know as late as ten or eleven o'clock. His mind was not fully made up until after he came back from Ewell's front . . . and had made the final examination on the right.

General Patrick Cleburne, Confederate Army

The war that has been bad is being waged on the military record of James Longstreet. It is not in keeping, in our opinion, with the record as is made up from the reports of General Lee, commander in chief of the Confederate Army in that conflict. If General Longstreet had failed to execute the orders of General Lee, and been the cause of the defeat of the Confederate Army, as is charged, we believe he would have been court-martialed and dismissed from the service instead of being retained and trusted on down to Appomattox, as he was.

Nevertheless, many of Lee's officers said that he was very frustrated with everything Longstreet did on the morning of July 2.

Douglas Southall Freeman, historian

Lee's one positive order was delivered at 11:00 o'clock for Longstreet to attack.

General James Longstreet

[Lee] informed me that it would not do to have Ewell open the attack. He finally determined that I should make the main attack on the extreme right.

Longstreet finally had some orders.

General James Longstreet

I received instructions from the commanding General to move, with the portion of my command that was up, around to gain the Emmitsburg Road, on the enemy left.

General Ambrose P. Hill, Confederate Army

Longstreet was to attack the left flank of the enemy and sweep down his line.

In a postwar letter to Longstreet, General Hood recalled:

General John Bell Hood, Confederate Army

The instructions I received were to place my division across and attack up the Emmitsburg Road.

Longstreet, in short, was to make a flanking attack on Union forces. Still, he was slow to act.

Captain William Goldsborough, in General Ewell's corps

Longstreet was slow, unaccountably slow. Had he attacked in the early morning, as he was expected to do, the enemy would have been driven from his strong position.

While Longstreet was incurring Lee's wrath for questioning his orders, Union general Daniel Sickles was taking things into his own hands. He decided to disobey orders and moved all his men to a different spot on the battlefield, near the Peach Orchard. It was just one example of troop movements made without higher authority.

He did this because he anticipated a Confederate attack on the left side of the long Union line, not its center. One of his aides explained.

Major H. E. Tremain, Union Army

Our Corps opened the fight. We knew where the battle would begin. I felt certain, for I told General Sickles on Wednesday night (as I had been over the ground more and had therefore better opportunities for knowing) that if the enemy attacked the army at all in its present position, it would be on the certain localities on the left, which I designated, and on Thursday morning he examined the topography and agreed with me. It was then he pressed on General Meade the necessity for changing his lines to meet such an anticipated attack. It was in that very locality, and by the roads I designated, that the enemy did come and hurl upon us their tremendous force.

This made the fierce fighting at the Peach Orchard and Devil's Den on day two all due to Sickles's impatience. Meade got on his horse at this news and rode directly to the Peach Orchard, where he ordered Sickles to return to his former position. An irate and highly agitated Sickles refused to leave. He told Meade that a huge Confederate attack was certain to take place and that it was going to be difficult to leave the Peach Orchard.

Captain William Paine, General Meade's aide

I never saw General Meade so angry. In a few sharp words . . . [he told Sickles] to rejoin his men.

General Humphreys's division then moved forward to an exposed position, a half-mile in front of Cemetery Hill. General Sickles's men were soon hit with a huge army of Confederates. That army extended from the Peach Orchard to the two Round Tops to the Emmitsburg Road.

General George Meade
The enemy threw immense masses on General Sickles's corps which, advanced and isolated in that way, it was not in my power to support promptly.

General McLaws's division converged on Humphreys's position. Sickles was wounded by then, and General David Birney ordered Humphreys to form a new line to the rear. Humphreys took his men close to the top of Cemetery Hill amid heavy fire. Humphreys rode up and down his line, encouraging his men to continue the hopeless assault. He and his men were stopped many times, but kept on moving.

General Andrew Humphreys
Twenty times did I bring my men to a halt and face about to fire myself & [members of my staff], forcing the men to do it, too.

Humphreys constantly put himself in danger to do this.

General Humphreys's aide
[He stayed] at the most exposed positions in the extreme front, giving personal attention to all the movements of the Division [with] conspicuous courage and remarkable coolness.

Meade could not fire on the Confederates without hitting his own men. What Meade did do, successfully, was order thousands of men from nearby divisions to move toward the Peach Orchard and bail out General Sickles and his trapped men. These men lost their way across the battlefield but did wind up fighting the enemy at the Peach Orchard, Devil's Den, and also at the Wheatfield that day.

The troops admired Meade for his sudden and emergency decisions that afternoon.

Major H. E. Tremain, Union Army
As I rode away, of one thing I felt assured, and that was that our army commander was then fully alive to the crisis of the situation, and that he was earnestly minded to do everything in his power to uphold our battle lines.

During that afternoon, Meade, on horseback, visited as many sites on the battlefield as he could, each time getting closer and closer to the heavy fire between both sides. At one point, a bullet cut through the leg of his pants, although it did not wound his leg. During the heavy fighting, he found himself riding up alongside General John Newton's division. Waving his hat and shouting as loudly as he could to be heard over the roar of the battle, he yelled:

General George Meade
Come on, gentlemen, come on!

A frightened soldier close to him yelled that the situation seemed imminently dangerous.

General George Meade
Yes, but it is all right now. It is all right now!

And, indeed, it was. General Alpheus Williams met with Meade and several other generals in a mini-conference on the battlefield. He later wrote his daughter:

General Alpheus Williams, Union Army

It was fast growing darker as late afternoon unfolded and the battle was really over. I chanced, however, to meet General Meade and a good many other officers on the field and to learn we had successfully resisted all the rebel attacks and had punished them severely. . . . There was a pleasant gathering in an open field and gratification and congratulation abounded.

The fighting at the Peach Orchard, while a crisis for the Union, pleased the Confederates. Longstreet was in overall charge of the Confederates at the Peach Orchard and Little Round Top, and was satisfied with the confrontations there, particularly the spirited advance of Hood's division.

General James Longstreet

[It] was the best three hours fighting ever done by any troops on any battlefield.

Shortly afterward, still in the Peach Orchard, Sickles's leg was shattered on a cannonball blast and had to be removed. By late afternoon, with plans gone wrong on both sides, the entire area of Gettysburg was fully engaged in battle.

Around that time, the Battle of Gettysburg was nearly lost for the Union when General Meade was almost killed—by, of all things, his runaway horse. An unexploded shell landed near Meade and spooked his horse. The horse began to run, uncontrollably, charging past artillery batteries, sharpshooters, and supply wagons. Meade, a fine horseman, took a long time to calm his horse down and they finally stopped. Meade had to think of the irony of the day: There were shells exploding all around him, tens of thousands of enemy soldiers ready to pounce on him, and he nearly gets killed by his horse.

An Engineer?

There was confusion all around. Then came Lee's order to have an engineer, Lieutenant Colonel Samuel Johnston, lead Longstreet's division.

General James Longstreet

General Lee ordered Colonel Johnston of his engineer corps to lead and conduct decisions as the head of the column. My troops, therefore, moved forward under the guidance of a special officer of General Lee and with instructions to follow his directions. . . . Lee ordered the march and put it under his engineer officers so as to assure that the troops would move by the best route and encounter the least [opposition] in reaching the position designated by him for the attack . . . at the same time concealing the movements then under orders from view of the federals.

Longstreet and his fellow officers were enraged. An engineer?

Lee said later that Johnston was there merely to tag along, not to lead the march. No one agreed with Longstreet's view that he was being replaced by the engineer.

Robert Krick, historian

Longstreet decided to play an ugly game with the misguided Lee and with thousands of unfortunate soldiers and the destiny of a mighty battle, by taking the ludicrous position that Samuel Johnston really commanded the march. He was Lee's man on the spot and this wholly silly march and attack were Lee's idea, so let him have his way and then we'll just see who really knows best.

General Lafayette McLaws, Confederate Army
Lee was as calm and cool as I ever saw him and evidenced nothing in his manner to make me think for a moment that he had been thwarted in any movement by any delay on the part of anyone or from any other cause.

It was McLaws who turned out to be a great champion of Longstreet at Gettysburg. He said that no one could have been successful in that day two afternoon attack.

General Lafayette McLaws
Was it General Longstreet's duty, or would he have been justified, when he became aware that General Lee's order could not be obeyed, that the reconnaissance on which they were based, have halted his command, and going back to General Lee, inform him of the true status of the enemy and that his order of attack should be changed and it was not the best under the circumstances.

Here, McLaws not only defended Longstreet, but said that Lee's thinking on the Union line was all wrong and that his scouts tracking it, his best men, were all wrong, too.

It turned out that during most of the first two days at Gettysburg, the Rebels were wrong on Northern troop strength and position.

Colonel E. Porter Alexander, Confederate Army
Not only was the selection of the point of attack about as bad as possible, but there does not seem to have been any special thought given to the

matter. It seems to have been allowed almost to select itself as if it was a matter of no consequence.

Later on day two of the battle, Longstreet was as stern and implacable as always. He was near Colonel Alexander's cannon and artillerists. They were firing at General Sickles's Union men just a few hundred yards in front of them. All was noise and smoke and wind and general mayhem. Longstreet was not scared, not one bit.

A soldier quite near him was thrilled.

Captain Decimus et Ultimus Barziza, 4th Texas Infantry

[Longstreet was] sitting on his horse like an iron man with his spyglass to his eye, coolly watching the effect of our shots. Limbs of trees fell and crashed around him, yet he sat as unmoved as a statue.

Little Round Top

A large Southern force was attacking Little Round Top through the thick woods. Union Colonel Joshua Chamberlain and his men from the 20th Maine were not only outnumbered but were down to the last reserves of their ammunition. Throughout the woods, Union soldiers could hear a sing-song-like sound—*pop, pop, pop*—from Confederate rifles and pistols, always getting closer. Union officers on the hill also assumed, from the sounds of gunfire, that the Confederates were coming through the woods all over Little Round Top and that they would soon be completely surrounded. Defeat seemed certain.

◆

Late in the afternoon of the second day, Union generals discovered that Little Round Top, one of two round-top hills on the battlefield, was wide open. If the Confederates could move through it uninterrupted, they could effectively attack the Union forces.

On top of Little Round Top with six pieces of artillery was Lieutenant Charles Hazlett—wearing a white straw hat. He'd been ordered there by Union general Gouverneur Warren. Warren was struck by the sight of Hazlett, a strange, singular figure in the middle of what might soon become a turning point in the battle—if the Confederates, as expected, could take it. Hazlett and his men had maneuvered the guns by hand up the rocky slope, exposed to Confederate fire the whole way. But on that steep slope, they could not operate the artillery effectively.

General Gouverneur Warren
This is no place for artillery fire.

Lieutenant Charles Hazlett
Never mind that. The sound of my guns will be encouraging to our troops and disheartening to the others, and my battery of no use if this hill is lost.

General Gouverneur Warren
[Hazlett was] the impersonation of valor and heroic beauty.

General Warren rode around the hill that was Little Round Top and saw that several regiments of Union troops—the 44th New York, 83rd Pennsylvania, 20th Maine, and 16th Michigan—had spread themselves out in a semicircle on the southern face of the hill to hold off the Confederates.

A reporter for the *New York Tribune* followed Warren around that afternoon.

Reporter, *New York Tribune*
[Warren] performed his duties in a most gallant and heroic manner, riding with the utmost confidence over fields swept by the enemy's fire . . . seemingly everywhere present, directing, aiding, and cheering the troops.

Warren worried about the 20th Maine. Its young commander, Colonel Joshua Chamberlain, had no substantial war experience. Prior to the war, he had been a professor of rhetoric at Bowdoin College in Maine, and had no military experience at all.

Chamberlain may have thought that about himself, but the warm reception he and his men received on their march to Gettysburg buoyed his spirits.

Colonel Joshua Chamberlain, Union Army
My men moved out [to Gettysburg] with a promptitude and spirit extraordinary, the cheers and welcome they received on the road adding to their enthusiasm.

When they arrived at Little Round Top, Colonel Strong Vincent of the 83rd Pennsylvania rode in front of Chamberlain and the men from Maine and yelled to them from his horse.

Colonel Strong Vincent, Union Army
I place you here! This is the left of the Union line. You understand! You are to hold this ground at all costs.

Vincent's voice was so dramatic that a brigade bugler got off his horse, found a rifle, and joined the defensive Union line. The enemy was on its way and getting closer to the 83rd Pennsylvania—two regiments from Alabama and two from Texas—coming through the thick woods slowly. The 48th Alabama found a field of rocks and got behind them, then opened fire on the Pennsylvanians.

Chamberlain's men in the 20th Maine watched hundreds of Rebels moving through the woods to their left. They expected a ferocious attack, and his men kept looking around, straining to see what was happening. It was late afternoon. It was hot. Very hot. Chamberlain had never been in a situation like this before. He spaced his men every five or ten yards and told them to prepare to fire. He was hoping this spacing would make his line long enough to hold back any size line the Confederates threw at him.

The battle started right away as the regiments from Alabama came close and fired. The entire area was soon filled with smoke from all the firing. After the war, several Union soldiers said that the smoke was so thick that they could only see the Rebels' legs.

Private Theodore Gerrish, 20th Maine

[I remember] how rapidly the cartridges were torn from the boxes and stuffed in the smoking muzzles of the guns. How the steel rammers clashed and clanged in the heated barrels, how the men's hands and faces grew grim and black with burning powder . . . the terrible medley of shouts, cheers, groans, prayers, curses, bursting shells, whizzing riddle-bullets, and clanging steel.

The Alabamians massed into a large unit and attacked Chamberlain's men, filling the hill with the rebel yell. Rookie commander Chamberlain, afraid he and his troops would be overrun, had an idea. He told his men to mass together in a close line. They would swing in a semicircle, bayonets fixed, and go down the hill quickly, attacking from one end of that "swinging gate" to the other. The bayonet charge, Chamberlain believed, would surprise and startle the Alabamians. They would not fight back, but flee.

Colonel Joshua Chamberlain

[The order to attack] ran like fire along the line, from man to man, and rose like a shout, with which they sprang forward upon the enemy, not thirty yards away.

He was right. Chamberlain's men executed the "swinging gate" charge down the hill beautifully and simply stunned the Southerners, who never expected a head-on assault. The Confederates were taken completely by surprise.

Colonel Joshua Chamberlain

The rebels seemed petrified with astonishment that their front line scarcely offered to run or fight. Hundreds of them fled and many were shot or stabbed in the tumult. The entire southern line collapsed and fled, with [our] men in hot pursuit.

The Union troops killed and wounded as many Rebels as they could—hundreds—and chased the rest away, running down the hill. The Rebels turned their backs on the Union line and ran as fast as they could. Many simply dropped their rifles and fled. That part of the hill had—surprisingly—been cleared by Chamberlain's dramatic charge.

Many of Chamberlain's men, now acting as sharpshooters, began picking off the Confederates as they fled. A minute or two later, as they ran, other infantrymen from the Union Army caught up with them, firing as they ran after the Rebels, and killing many. The Rebels were all pushed off Little Round Top.

It was a complete and totally unexpected victory for the Federals. The Confederates never again tried to take the hill. The countercharge with bayonets by Chamberlain made the professor an instant national hero. Upon his return to Maine after the war, he was elected Maine's governor several times.

Little Round Top had been held, and that was a key to the Union victory that day. The cost of victory for the Federals had been high, though. General Stephen Weed, Colonel Strong Vincent, Lieutenant Charles Hazlett, and Colonel Patrick O'Rorke of the 140th New York were killed. Of the 2,996 Union soldiers engaged there on July 2, 134 were killed, 402 wounded, and 29 missing. Southern casualties were even higher. Of its 4,864 soldiers there, 279 were killed, 868 wounded, and 219 missing. Southern general John Bell Hood was badly wounded that day in fighting nearby.

The victory at Little Round Top solidified the Union hold on the field that day, but there was fierce fighting in many other places, such as the Peach Orchard and Devil's Den. Throughout the field, the chaos of the battle forced many commanders (like Chamberlain) to make decisions they did not want to make, but did—and successfully. This happened on both sides.

◆

Southerners claimed for years that the confrontation might not even have happened if General Longstreet had attacked in the morning, as planned, and not in the afternoon. If he had attacked Little Round Top before noon, they said, he and his men might have taken and held it.

Colonel E. Porter Alexander, Confederate Army
It has since appeared that if our corps had made its attack even if two or three hours sooner than it did our chances of success would have been immensely increased . . . ten or eleven o'clock at the latest it was entirely practicable for us to have delivered our attack in good shape.

Alexander blamed Longstreet.

Colonel E. Porter Alexander
Longstreet did not wish to take the offensive. His objection to it was not based at all upon the peculiar strength of the enemy's position, for that was not yet recognized, but solely upon general principles.

Historian James McPherson agreed.

James McPherson, historian
Longstreet's state of mind as he prepared for this attack is hard to fathom . . . but Longstreet did seem to move slowly at Gettysburg.

Although Lee wanted him to attack as early in the day as possible, he did not get his troops into position until 4:00 P.M.

Longstreet may have been piqued by Lee's rejection of his flanking suggestion, and he did not believe in the attack he was ordered to make. He therefore might not have put as much energy and speed into its preparation as the situation required.

Historian Douglas Southall Freeman always believed that Longstreet was angry at Lee for turning down his own battle plan.

Douglas Southall Freeman, historian
[Longstreet] sulked. In plain, ugly words, he sulked. The dissent of Longstreet's mind was a brake on his energies. . . . There can be no escaping the conclusion that his behavior was that of a man who sulked because his plan was rejected by his chief.

Shelby Foote, historian
Renewing [Longstreet's] pleas for a withdrawal this morning, the burly Georgian had been rebuffed again, whereupon he turned sulky. Although he had, of course, obeyed all orders given him, he had not anticipated them in the best tradition of the Army of Northern Virginia, with the result that he was partly to blame for the delays encountered.

The Wheatfield

By 4:30 P.M. or so, the battle moved to a different place on the huge battlefield. In the north-central area, a peach orchard stood in the middle of the grounds and a large wheat field was situated next to it. The Wheatfield covered slightly more than nineteen acres and was owned by George Rose. The Confederates believed that the acres of huge, thick stalks of wheat could offer some protection, and slowly crept into it as the sun began to slide down over the horizon.

The Southerners were from Georgia and were led by Brigadier General George Anderson. They ran into Federal troops behind a stone wall alongside the southern boundary of the Wheatfield. A hot battle ensued, but the Federals could offer little resistance because most were either out of ammunition or their ammunition had run pretty low.

Meade was angry because earlier he had ridden around the area and seen the formation of a long, substantial Confederate troop line and noticed that they were starting to move toward the Wheatfield. Meade knew about how many Union men were in the field and knew that the Confederates would overwhelm them.

Meade was close to Little Round Top when Lieutenant Washington Roebling galloped up to give him news of the fighting there.

Lieutenant Washington Roebling, Union Army, riding from the Wheatfield

I rode quickly over to General Meade, explained the situation, gave him at least a ray of confidence, and then returned.

It was late in the day, and Meade, aware of the entire situation, decided to do something dangerous—take command of the entire Wheatfield force himself. Meade stayed where he was, a spot from which he could monitor several battles at the same time, including the action in the Wheatfield.

He found General George Sykes nearby and told him to throw his entire corps into the support of General David Birney and his men in the Wheatfield, whom, Meade knew, could never hold off the impending Confederate attack.

General George Meade

Throw [your] whole corps to that point [with Birney's men] and hold it at all costs.

A short time later, Sykes met Brigadier General James Barnes. As they talked, General Gouverneur Warren rode up and asked Sykes for men to help him secure Little Round Top, where Confederate soldiers had started to move up the hill. They dispatched Colonel Vincent to bring several hundred of his men up to the top of Little Round Top. A short time after that, Colonel Patrick O'Rorke and his men rode down the road and were also directed to Little Round Top, greatly assisting Colonel Joshua Chamberlain in the fierce fighting there.

General Stephen Weed's men were similarly turned around and sent to Little Round Top, a short distance from the Wheatfield. They were too late to help—the battle on the hill had already been won.

Meade was then directed to a nearby field hospital to get some water on that very hot afternoon. There, he met Tillie Pierce, who had just arrived after leaving her home, which was under siege by the Confederates. Hearing of the general's desire for a cup of water, she procured a battered tin cup and filled it with water. She apologized to Meade for the condition of the cup.

General George Meade
Certainly, that is all right.

Nervous laughter followed. Meade gave the cup back to the girl and thanked her again.

He stood to go outside and get on his horse. With no direction from anyone, dozens of men in the field hospital clapped their hands and screamed out:

Union Soldiers in a field hospital
Three cheers for General Meade!

As Meade rode off, Union lines in places within the Wheatfield collapsed. As Meade had predicted, General Birney's line weakened under the intense Confederate assault, and the cannons Birney had moved from the Peach Orchard to the Wheatfield had a good position but no infantry support. Confederate fire grew in intensity.

Lieutenant Malbone Watson and his 5th U.S. Artillery Battery seemed trapped at the edge of the Wheatfield and heavy cannon fire threatened them all.

Union soldier
Watson's men and horses were shot down or disabled to such an extent that the [battery] was virtually abandoned.

Union soldier

All at once, our line was swept by an enfilading fire under which no troops could remain and live, and it became necessary to fall back without the range of the deadly hail. We were losing very heavily in our regiment but fell back in good order, contesting stubbornly every inch of the ground.

One officer suddenly discovered that the Confederates he thought he had chased off the field were back again at the other end of it, now attacking Union men in the Peach Orchard.

Numerous men and horses died there under the heavy fire from the enemy. One captain lost forty of his horses there.

Lieutenant Colonel Freeman McGilvery, under steady pressure, told another officer he was all for retreating.

Lieutenant Colonel Freeman McGilvery, Union Army

All of Sickles's men have withdrawn and [I] am alone on the field. I have no support of any kind. [Line] up and get out.

Captain John Bigelow, to McGilvery

If you attempted to do so, the [Confederate] sharpshooters on your left front would shoot [all your men] down.

The fight in the Wheatfield had turned ferocious.

Private Robert Carter, 22nd Massachusetts

[T]he screaming and bursting of shells, canister and shrapnel with their swishing sound as they tore through the struggling masses of humanity, the death screaming of wounded animals, the groans of their human companions, wounded and dying, are trampled underfoot by hurrying batteries, riderless horses and the moving lines of battle, all coming in an indescribable roar of discordant elements—in fact, a perfect hell on

earth. . . . the unalterable horror, implacable, unyielding, full of sorrow, heartbreaks, untold sufferings, wretched longings, doubts and fears . . . nothing could live before such a fire.

Late in the afternoon, Union general Régis de Trobriand's brigade was attacked while they recovered behind a stone wall along the southern side of the Wheatfield. Trobriand's men held back that initial assault, but the Confederates tried again. This time they attacked with cannon firing away and Trobriand's men retreated. Then cannon from a New York brigade opened up on the Confederates and mowed down hundreds of them.

Over the next hour or so, Confederates bombarded the middle of the Union line, disfiguring it. At the same time, a second Confederate horde of soldiers arrived and the Federals were hit from both sides.

....

Lieutenant John Garden, 62nd Pennsylvania

The bullets were whistling all the time. . . .

[Later, Colonel William] Tilton's brigade was driven out of the woods on our right and the enemy flanked us, but we kept our ground until orders came to fall back, and then we about-faced in order, firing as we fell back, but it was an awful place. Many men fell, for a time it looked like a panic. The regiment lost four officers killed and nine wounded. Also, another 21 men killed and 99 wounded and 75 missing. The brigade—only three regiments then, lost 34 officers and 582 men.

Meanwhile, cannons from different regiments were collected and moved to the top of the Wheatfield, where they fired upon the Confederates. The Confederates fired back from different angles. As it became darker, regiments with both men and cannon attacked one another.

The darkness grew, and a massive Union force attacked the Confederates in the Wheatfield. The first Minnesota was one of the first regiments in the attack.

Colonel William Colvill, First Minnesota
Charge!

Captain Henry C. Coates, also of the First Minnesota, described fighting the Alabamians in the Confederate line.

Captain Henry C. Coates, First Minnesota
The fire we encountered was terrible. Even so, we inflicted severe punishment upon the enemy, and stopped his advance. We there lost in killed and wounded about two-thirds of our men and officers who were engaged.

Colvill was severely wounded in the attack. Seven company commanders were killed. Altogether, nearly two-thirds of the Union soldiers in that fight were killed or lay wounded on the field. The Wheatfield was lost, for that hour.

It was at this point that General Meade arrived. He was aghast. Shortly afterward, an officer there ordered a fast-paced bayonet charge. That move surprised the Confederates, who backed away fast. Union officers regrouped their men quickly and ordered a countercharge that pushed back the Southerners.

As General Meade watched the Union slowly recover its position, he was again nearly killed. A bullet cut into his trouser leg, missed his right leg, and crashed into his saddle. That was the second time at Gettysburg that he had come so close to death.

Shortly after that, troops from Maine drove troops from Georgia out of the Wheatfield. Meade then ordered the newly arrived Sixth Corps to get into the fight. The fresh troops did, and with a vengeance. They tore into the Confederates again and again and, in darkness, pretty much pushed them out of the Wheatfield.

North and South fought each other for over an hour before both sides left the Wheatfield. Losses on both sides there were considerable: The Union and Confederates engaged some 20,000 men in that part of the battle and each side suffered about 30 percent casualties. Each side lost a general, too; Brigadier General Paul Semmes, on the Southern side, was shot early in the action. He was taken to a field hospital nearby but died six days later, after much pain and suffering. The Union lost Brigadier General Samuel Zook, who had marched his men into battle over the bodies of dozens of dead Union soldiers. As he did so, he was shot in the stomach by a Confederate. General Zook died just after midnight that evening. The losses on both sides at the Wheatfield were among the heaviest of the battle's three days.

Culp's Hill

Culp's Hill was a topographical mess. It was full of thick woods, ravines, severe slopes, and dozens of clusters of large boulders that men could hide behind. On July 2 and the morning of July 3 it was held by the Union, with soldiers scrambling for cover on it behind the rocks and trees.

On July 2, early in the morning, both sides exchanged rifle fire for long periods. The hill was held by Meade's 12th Corps, whose men were firmly entrenched. Around daybreak, Confederate general Ewell's men attacked Culp's Hill. They advanced slowly through the rough terrain. The Union had numerous cannon batteries that opened fire. The South had few.

Some Union commanders were convinced that Ewell's assault was a diversionary tactic to draw attention away from a larger, concentrated attack that would start in the early afternoon. Ewell saw it differently: Lee had sent him to take Culp's Hill and he assumed that was a singular mission for him and his men. He had little information about what the Confederate Army would do that afternoon. For Ewell, his attack on Culp's Hill was the major contest that day and perhaps of the entire battle.

Ewell knew that the Confederates had already seized small sections of the hill and were hard to dislodge, despite the blustery order of Union general Henry Slocum the night before about the Rebels: "Hell, drive them out at daylight."

When daylight came on July 2, Union soldiers found that the Confederates were in charge of many spots on Culp's Hill and seemed to have an advantage, despite careful defensive planning by Meade and the Union.

The night before, Colonel George Greene correctly assessed the challenge to the Confederates in their woods and rock formations.

Colonel George Greene, Union Army

Until they got us out of it, [the Confederates] could not safely move forward. Besides, we could work along the line on that flank.

The Union formed a long line that started at the top of the hill and ran down its center and was as strong defensively as the Southern positions.

At about 4:30 A.M., just as the sun was about to rise, the Union artillery on the hill opened fire on the Rebels, some as close as 2,400 feet from the top of the hill. The cannonade was nonstop for a full fifteen minutes.

If the Southerners were surprised, they did not show it. Their artillery fired back, hard, right after the Union shelling ceased.

General Alpheus Williams, Union Army

On the discontinuance of the fire, the enemy, without waiting for our assault, themselves attacked Geary's division with great fury.

The Union fired back. This small battle grew, at Meade's suggestion, so that the long line of Union guns continually fired at the Rebels, pinning many down in their positions.

General Marsena Patrick, Union Army

A large share of the Union success that day [was due to the heavy artillery fire].

The Rebel guns had their share of success as well. The 2nd Massachusetts was turned back after heavy fire at short distance. Its attack failed but was applauded by General Williams.

General Alpheus Williams
There are few, if any, regiments in the service that could withstand the almost instantaneous loss of half its forces & maintained, as the 2nd Massachusetts did . . . perfectly the order and regularity of a battlefield drill.

Following six hours of close fighting, the Rebels gave up Culp's Hill and retreated.

General Alpheus Williams
The wonder is that the rebels persisted so long in an attempt that in the first half hour must have seemed useless.

Late that afternoon, Meade received reports that a Confederate Army was moving on his left. He would have to once again change his plans.

General George Meade wrote to General Halleck:
I have today, up to this hour awaited the attack of the enemy. I have a strong position for the defensive. I am not determined on attacking him. The army is fatigued.

Fighting on the late afternoon of the second day of the battle was fierce, but cut short by darkness. General Longstreet was supposed to attack the center of Cemetery Hill, joined by other forces.

General Armistead Long, General Lee's aide
I understood the plan of battle to be Longstreet, on the right, should commence the attack, while Hill, in the center, and Ewell, on the right, would co-operate by vigorous support.

But Longstreet did not see those forces nearby.

General James Longstreet
These two movements or extensions so drew my forces out that I found myself attacking Cemetery Hill with a single line of battle against no less than 50,000 troops.

Neither general had a complete army, and despite initial success by Longstreet's men, the attack failed.

Arthur Fremantle, British journalist
Longstreet carried everything before him for some time, capturing several batteries, and driving the enemy from his positions, but when Hill's Florida brigade and some other troops gave way, he was forced to abandon a small portion of the ground he had won, along with all the captured guns, except three.

General Early wrote after the war that Lee had never directly ordered him to advance with Longstreet, and pointed the finger at Longstreet.

General Jubal Early
Ewell was to make a demonstration upon the enemy's right, to be converted into a real attack should the opportunity offer—that is, should success attend the attack on the enemy's left. . . . [Because] Longstreet attacked

late in the afternoon . . . there could not be that cooperation that would have taken place had the attack been promptly made at the expected time.

Colonel E. Porter Alexander blamed everybody.

Colonel E. Porter Alexander, Confederate Army
Longstreet's attack between 4:00 P.M. and darkness by the other two corps was confined to an artillery duel by 32 guns of Ewell and 55 of Hill, mostly at extreme ranges. But the value of this duel as assistance to Longstreet was absolutely nothing. For it did not prevent the enemy from withdrawing troops from every corps in his line to repel our assault.

General Lee saw day two at Gettysburg as a victory. General Longstreet did not.

General James Longstreet
The conflict had been fierce and bloody and my troops had driven back heavy columns and had encountered a force three or four times their number, but we had accomplished little towards victorious results.

Glenn Tucker, historian
Whether from lack of experience in high command or lack of innate ability, the shortcomings of Ewell and A. P. Hill were critical. Compared with them, the deficiencies of Longstreet were indeed venial.

Many Southerners blamed Longstreet for the lack of victory on day two, citing his late start and his lack of confidence in the plan for the attack. He always said it was not his fault and that, given the circumstances, Lee should not have put him in charge on day two.

General James Longstreet

[Lee] knew that I did not believe success was possible, that care and time should be taken to give the troops the benefit of positions and the grounds, and he should have put an officer in charge who had more confidence in his plan. Two thirds of the troops were from other commands, and there was no reason for putting the assaulting forces under my charge.

Devil's Den

Devil's Den was a nickname used to describe the Gettysburg Sill, a large area filled with huge, odd-shaped boulders and little else. The term started to be used right after the first shots were fired because of the ferocity of the fight there and the extraordinary number of casualties on both sides.

The Union Army under General Sickles got there after a dispute between Sickles and Meade over where Sickles should take his men. The Rebels got there following a twenty-minute artillery bombardment, courtesy of the 4th New York Independent artillery battery commanded by Captain James Smith.

It was Confederate general John Bell Hood's men in the front of the Rebel attack. The two forces, of around 3,000 men each, met in one of the fiercest battles at Gettysburg that day.

The large boulders of Devil's Den made walking and running quite difficult. Men on both sides complained of the rocks and the difficulty of firing rifles on that ground. So many soldiers were killed in place that it was immediately nicknamed "the slaughter pen."

Houck's Ridge ran through Devil's Den, and the Union soldiers defending it were met with a strong Southern charge that pushed them back. Regiments from Alabama and Texas swarmed into Devil's Den, seizing it, but found it impossible to hold because there was little protection for them in the rocks. They withdrew and then attacked

Devil's Den a second time. This time their charge was successful and the Rebels held the Den all day.

On the Southern side, as on the Northern side, mistakes were made. Confederate general Robert Rodes failed to meet up with General Ewell for a combined attack. Ewell was criticized by some for not launching his attack an hour or so earlier.

There were a lot of changed plans by the leaders on both sides throughout the day. One particularly angry officer was Union general Humphreys.

General Andrew Humphreys, Union Army

Had my division been left intact, I should have driven the enemy back. But this ruinous habit of putting troops in position & then drawing off its reserves & second line to help others, who if similarly disposed would need no such help, is disgusting.

It was a hard day for both sides. More than 1,800 men were killed, wounded, or captured at Devil's Den.

The fighting that day extended past nightfall, and as dark descended across Gettysburg men on both sides were lost and found themselves in fierce skirmishes with soldiers they could not see. General Humphreys and his men, who had fought hard all day, found themselves fighting at night, too, in very poor conditions. By 9:00 P.M. both sides, North and South, were uncertain where the enemy was.

Several military historians concluded that throughout the second day, commanders on both sides made poor decisions, many without full information about what the enemy was doing. Many commanders reported that when they did know what they were doing, early darkness canceled whatever plans they came up with.

Colonel Archibald Godwin, Confederate Army

In the charge up the hill, the command had become much separated and in the darkness it was now found impossible to concentrate more than 40 or 50 men at any point for a further advance.

Many men, both sides, stayed where they were, no matter where they were, and slept on their arms in groups or entire regiments that night. What would the morning bring?

No one knew.

A Long Night

The fighting that day had been intense, with some 16,000 casualties on both sides. The dead lay everywhere—under trees, next to brooks, in fields, hanging over fences. Union and Confederate troops made small fires for warmth and to enable men on both sides to see. What they saw was sad and sometimes shocking.

Union soldier
[The rebel dead] were piled in lines like windrows of hay.

J. B. Clifton, Confederate soldier
Longstreet's men slept on a field black with the enemy's killed and wounded.

Entire brigades had been punished severely.

Colonel Patrick Guiney, 9th Massachusetts, on a brigade he had joined that day
We could scarcely be said to join the brigades. It seemed to me that it would be more appropriate to say we constituted the brigade. There were the flags of the regiment and a remnant of a splendid regiment around

each & there were a few officers near their respective colors . . . [but] the brigade—except ourselves—had been fought nearly to extinction.

All was quiet at General Meade's headquarters on the night of July 2 as a dozen or so generals gathered. Someone offered Meade a drink of liquor but, as always, he refused. The officers had all been in battle and their jackets, covered with dirt, showed it. Then, all of a sudden, General George Sharpe arrived. Sharpe was head of the Bureau of Military Information. He and his staff were nowhere near any of the fighting at Gettysburg, yet all were surprised to see Sharpe's shabby condition.

Union observer

[Sharpe] was covered with dust and his face felt as though it had a thick incrustation of mud on it.

It seems that no one in the massive Union Army had escaped the battle that day.

Meade had asked General Butterfield to gather several generals so they could decide what to do on the next day. Critically, the army's rations were running very low, and Meade wondered if the entire army should move to an area closer to supply wagons or stay and fight and hope the battle would not last long.

No one knows how much food was left for the Union soldiers. The best guess among officers at that time was one day more, possibly two, even with the General Halleck's order to kill whatever animals—cattle especially—the soldiers could find.

For that matter, how much food did the Rebels have? One day's worth? Two days? Three?

The lack of food was an issue for everyone—one that has not been written about enough. At some point the rations would have all been devoured and all the cattle in the Gettysburg area would have been slaughtered—to the dismay of the local farmers. How long could the battle last with food in such short supply? Would not one army or the other simply have to surrender or flee?

General Daniel Butterfield, Union Army
Under existing circumstances, is it advisable for this army to remain in its present position, or to retire to another nearer its base of supplies?

The Union generals voted unanimously to remain in Gettysburg and carry the fight to its conclusion, no matter what that was.

Meade nodded his head.

General George Meade
Such, then, is the decision.

Meade wrote a short note to General Halleck in Washington to explain his plan for the third day of the battle.

General George Meade
The enemy attacked about 4:00 P.M. [today]. After one of the severest contests of the war, was repulsed at all points. We have suffered considerably in killed and wounded. Have taken a large number of prisoners. I shall remain in my present position tomorrow but am not prepared to say, until better advised of the condition of the Army, whether my operations will be of an offensive or defensive character.

Then Meade wrote to his wife. . . .

General George Meade
We had a great fight yesterday.

Of course, no one knew what General Lee had planned for July 3, the third day of the battle. Would he continue to engage in small fights here and there, hopeful that a large enough number of small victories would force the Federals back and into a disorganized retreat? Would Lee stage a huge attack of some kind, somewhere, looking to defeat the Federals in one powerful masterstroke?

Lee's men had not fared well in the first two days of fighting and the Union controlled all of the battlefield.

Edwin Coddington, historian
[Lee was troubled] by the loss of Stonewall Jackson, the departure of Stuart's cavalry, the uncertainty about Meade's intentions. Much of Lee's uneasiness undoubtedly arose from Longstreet's rather truculent attitude and obvious unwillingness to attack.

That night, at his headquarters, General Lee came up with a startling and astounding plan of attack for the next day. It would be unprecedented. It would be historic. It would be like nothing the commanders of either side had seen or even dreamed of.

It would bring victory, Lee was absolutely certain.

It came to be known as Pickett's Charge.

PART FOUR

July 3–Day Three of the Battle of Gettysburg

Late on the morning of July 3, Federal cannon fire, which had been roaring for hours, had just about ceased. General Lee, sitting on his white horse, Traveler, assumed that the Union gunners were running out of ammunition. He figured the Union must be low on ordinary firepower, too, such as revolver and rifle bullets, because the battle had been raging for nearly seventy-two hours and supplies everywhere were low.

The lack of cannon fire would enable him to send General George Pickett and his 12,500 men on a wild and historic charge straight up the steep Cemetery Hill into that army of blue, split it, and crush the Union forces that Lee assumed were low on ammunition.

That steamy hot morning, Lee issued his order with great confidence for General Pickett and his division to attack the center of the Federal line at top of the ridge.

....

General Robert E. Lee
The attack must succeed.

Lee's military secretary, General Armistead Long, said there was another reason, a technical one, as well.

General Armistead Long, Confederate Army

There was . . . a weak point . . . where Cemetery Hill sloping westward, formed the depression through which the Emmitsburg Road passes. Perceiving that by forcing the federal lines at that point and turning towards Cemetery Hill [Union general Alexander Hays's division] would be taken in the flank and the remainder would be neutralized. . . . Lee determined to attack at that point, using clumps of trees on a farm on top of the hill as a visual target for his soldiers. The execution was assigned to Longstreet, who would oversee Pickett and two other generals.

In his diary, Confederate soldier Randolph McKim described his army's setback that morning, well before Pickett's Charge. McKim and his men had been ordered to storm Culp's Hill in a second day of hard fighting there.

Lieutenant Randolph McKim, Confederate Army

The works to be stormed ran almost at right angles to those we occupied. Moreover, there was a double line of entrenchments, one above the other, and each filled with troops. In moving to the attack we were exposed to enfilading fire from the woods on our left flank, besides the double line of fire we had to face in front, and a battery of artillery posted on a hill to our left rear opened upon us at short range.

On swept the gallant little brigade, the third North Carolina, on the right side of the line, next the second Maryland then the three Virginia regiments (10th, 23rd and 37th) with the First North Carolina on the extreme left. Its ranks had been sadly thinned and its energies greatly depleted by those six fearful hours of battle that morning, but its nerve and spirit were undiminished. Soon, however, the left and center were checked and then repulsed, probably by the severe flank fire from the woods, and the small remnant of the Third North Carolina, with the stronger second Maryland (I do not recall the banners of any other regiment) were far in advance of the rest of the line. On they pressed to within about twenty or thirty paces of the works, a small but gallant band of heroes, daring to attempt what could not be done by flesh and blood.

The end soon came. We were beaten back to the place from which we had come with terrible loss, and in much confusion, but the enemy did not make a countercharge. By the strenuous efforts of the officers of the line and staff order was restored and we reformed in the breastworks from which we had emerged, there to be exposed to artillery fire exceeding in violence that of the early morning. It remained only to say that, like Pickett's men later in the day, this single brigade was hurled, unsupported, against the enemy's works. Daniels's brigade remained in the breastworks during and after the charge. And neither from that command or any other had we any support.

General Armistead Long

There had been difficult fighting all morning, well before Pickett's Charge, and things had not gone well for the South. Lee had ordered small attacks on different areas of the battlefield and perhaps the lack of coordination hurt his cause.

Why was Lee so hopeful about Pickett's Charge? He had not been able to defeat the North after two days of hard fighting. What made him think day three would be different? That Pickett's Charge would bring victory?

General "Old Pete" Longstreet, one of Lee's best generals, his second in command, was dead set against it. He had started protesting Lee's plan as far back as the beginning of May, and never changed his opinion. Longstreet had been against just about all of Lee's plans at Gettysburg, too. He thought Lee ought to be fighting defensive battles in Pennsylvania and make the enemy come to him and attack him. He told this to Lee and other officers several times, quietly, and had pleaded again and again, alone, with Lee, not to make the charge. Lee, however, incorrectly assumed that since Longstreet did not mightily and loudly disagree with the Gettysburg plans at numerous meetings, in front of all the commanders, that he was in fact in favor of his commander's tactics. He was not.

Lee had lost the marauding general J. E. B. Stuart somewhere out in the Pennsylvania farmlands, and now, by underestimating—or discounting—Longstreet's opposition to his plans for the attack at Gettysburg, had put the very tentative General Longstreet out on a limb. He would be depending on his number two man, Longstreet, to lead his army into a battle that Longstreet did not even believe should take place.

Lee met with Longstreet at 7:30 A.M. on the morning of July 3, the morning of Pickett's Charge, to talk over the plan for the charge. It is not known whether Lee chastised Longstreet for his slow movements on days one and two of the battle.

General Robert E. Lee

Longstreet is a very good fighter when he gets in position and gets everything ready, but he is so slow.

Longstreet later wrote in his memoirs about his objections to Lee's plan.

General James Longstreet

[Lee] rode over after sunrise and gave his orders. His plan was to assault the enemy's left center by a column to be composed of McLaws's and Hood's divisions reinforced by Pickett's brigades. I thought that it would not do; that the point had been fully tested the day before, by more men, when all were fresh; that the enemy was there looking for us, as we heard him during the night putting up his defenses; that the divisions of McLaws and Hood were holding a mile along the right of my line against twenty thousand men, who would follow their withdrawal, strike the flank of the assaulting column, crush it, and get on our rear towards the Potomac River; that thirty thousand men was the minimum of force necessary

for the work; that even such force would need close cooperation on other parts of the line; that the column as he proposed to organize it would have only about thirteen thousand men (the divisions having lost a third of their numbers the day before); that the column would have to march a mile under concentrating battery fire, and a thousand yards under long-range musketry; that the conditions were different from those in the days of Napoleon, when field batteries had a range of six hundred yards and musketry about sixty yards.

He said the distance was not more than fourteen hundred yards. General Meade's estimate was a mile or a mile and a half. He then concluded that the divisions of McLaws and Hood could remain on the defensive line; that he would reinforce by divisions of the Third Corps and Pickett's brigades, and stated the point to which the march should be directed. I asked the strength of the column. He stated fifteen thousand. Opinion was then expressed that the fifteen thousand men who could make a successful assault over that field had never been arrayed for battle; but he was impatient of listening, and tired of talking, and nothing was left but to proceed.

Lee was still full of that optimism he had gained at Chancellorsville. He was a great general, he told himself, and led a great army. It was the Confederacy that held the advantage that summer, not the Federals. If he could win at Chancellorsville, he could surely win at Gettysburg.

Pickett had just arrived, and all of his men were fresh troops. J. E. B. Stuart, his trusted cavalry commander, had finally arrived late in the afternoon the day before. Stuart was the best cavalry commander on either side, and that morning he was lusting for a fight. They outgunned the Union, 160-some cannons to, Lee assumed, less than 100. All the necessary elements were in place, Lee told Longstreet. His men, who had fought so hard, wanted and needed a victory, and that would come through Pickett's Charge.

A victory at Gettysburg would change the course of the war and give Lee's officers and men enormous confidence. In addition to all that, Lee knew that his men loved him. He loved them, and a victory at Gettysburg would be a nice way to bring an end to this war and a great triumph for him and all his troops.

Lee and his men still tasted that victory at Chancellorsville. They were invincible. The general and many of his men thought so. Many of the Federals did, too.

On the other side of the battlefield, General Meade had no worries about his generals and colonels. Everything ran smoothly and they were all with him. The Union army had been victorious in just about all the skirmishes the previous day and, this morning, July 3, held all of the battlefield—with strength. Meade expected the Rebels to do something important on the third day at Gettysburg but did not know what they would do. There had been some early morning cannon fire here and there, but nothing substantial. He had reports of early morning musket fire on different places on the battlefield, but did not know, could not know, the significance of that.

The previous day, July 2, had been a day of difficult fighting for Lieutenant Abner Small of the 16th Maine, who had been engaged since noon in fierce battle with the enemy on Oak Ridge. They had been ordered to hold their position at all costs, to cover a strategic withdrawal. Today, things were a lot quieter.

Lieutenant Abner Small, 16th Maine adjutant

At daylight of July 3rd, we were withdrawn and moved up to the left. As we came up the hill, we heard to the east the boom of cannon on the morning air; a little later we heard musketry; and by snatches we caught the noise of fighting until late in the fore noon. Near us, all was quiet. Colonel [Richard] Coulter established brigade headquarters on the brow of the hill, at the left of the cemetery, pitching his tent in the edge of a small grove of trees and planting defiantly in full sight of the rebels the brigade flag.

From this point I could see almost all the Union position from Cemetery Hill to the Round Tops, two miles to the south, and the opposing curve of Seminary Ridge, now held by the rebels, and the valley between. The skirmish lines in the valley were clearly defined by streaks of curling smoke that faced upwards in the shimmering heat. A false calm possessed the field.

Dozens of Confederate troops had been moved from one place to another, but from Meade's point of view, there was no design to the third day's morning movements. The only thing he knew for sure about day three at Gettysburg was that it was hot—scorching hot—and the heat showed no signs of letting up. He, and everybody else, had to endure it.

The shy Meade accepted an invitation from General Gibbon to join him and some other generals and senior officers for a chicken lunch. As Meade and the others ate and the time approached noon, the weather became excessively hot—so hot that one could hardly breathe. General Meade finished his lunch sitting on an empty food crate. Meade talked about the general stalemate of the previous two days and wondered, along with everyone else, what the Confederates would do on day three.

Shortly after noon, Meade mounted his horse and rode off to inspect different areas of the battlefield, including Little Round Top, where his men, under Colonel Joshua Chamberlain, had held off the Rebels all afternoon on the previous day before finally defeating them with a heroic, unprecedented bayonet charge. There, he met General Warren and they discussed the heroics of Chamberlain and his men. Then Meade galloped off to inspect a few other battlefield sites before returning to his headquarters.

1:00 P.M.

2:00 P.M.

Nothing yet. Deep inside, Meade sensed that something very, very dramatic was going to take place—and soon.

Meade asked his aides, "What will they do?"

"Where?"

Pickett's Charge

General George Pickett's position that morning was an oddity. He was a recent arrival. He and his men, assigned to other duties, did not arrive in Gettysburg until the end of the second day's battle. They were fresh to the battle, but unfamiliar with the town and its rolling farmland surroundings, and with the two-day battle itself.

Pickett himself was an unusual general. He had graduated last in his class at West Point back in 1846, esteemed by no one, and yet had turned out to be a pretty good general.

Pickett was one of eight children of a prominent Virginia family, and always wanted to be a soldier. He was thrown into combat in the Mexican War, right after graduation, and impressed all. Lieutenant James Longstreet, wounded at the Battle of Chapultepec in the Mexican War in 1847, handed the colors to Pickett. Pickett led a charge, carried the colors over the wall, and forced the Mexicans there to surrender. He was promoted to captain. He married Sally Minge, who died shortly thereafter.

Pickett then supervised the construction of a US fort at Bellingham, Washington, and married a Haida Nation woman, Morning Mist. She died a few months after giving birth to their son.

In 1861, when the Civil War began, Pickett was in the state of Washington. He informed his commander that he wanted to resign his US Army commission and join the Confederates, and was told he could only do that in Washington, DC, more than three thousand miles away. Pickett then sailed on a small steamer from Tacoma, Washington, to Panama, trekked forty miles across the country to the Gulf of Mexico, sailed from there to Richmond, and then, very tired, went to Washington, DC, to resign.

Pickett performed well for the Confederates in the battles of Williamsburg, Seven Pines, and others. He was wounded in an assault at Gaines' Mill and tried to continue the charge, leading his horse and his men on foot. He was out of action for three months and his arm did not heal for nearly a year. He was promoted to general in October 1862, at age thirty-seven, but missed the Chancellorsville battle just before Gettysburg.

In the spring of 1863, Pickett fell in love with LaSalle "Sallie" Corbell, who was eighteen years younger than him, and rode frequently to visit her, angering his superiors.

George Pickett was a flamboyant general, and a dandy if there ever was one. He could easily be recognized by his small blue cap and his wildly flowing ringlets of hair that were not only meticulously cut, but scented with perfume, as was his goatee. His full moustache and well-groomed beard impressed all. He wore an immaculately tailored uniform with two rows of bright gold buttons and buffed gloves. He added shiny gold spurs to his army boots and polished them often. His care of his horse, Old Black, became legendary. He carried an elegant riding crop wherever he went, on his horse or just walking around the army camp.

Lieutenant Colonel Moxley Sorrel, one of Pickett's aides, described his flamboyant boss well.

Lieutenant Colonel Moxley Sorrel, Confederate Army

He was a medium-sized, well-built man, straight, erect and in well-fitting uniform, an elegant riding whip in his hand, his appearance was distinguished.

Long ringlets flowed loosely over his shoulders, trimmed and highly perfumed; his beard likewise was curling and giving out the scents of Araby.

Ralph Moses, Confederate chief commissary officer
He was foppish in his dress.

Arthur Fremantle, British journalist
He wears his hair in long ringlets and is altogether a desperate looking character.

When women throughout Virginia and Pennsylvania asked Lee for a lock of his hair, Lee, smiling, refused, and referred them to Pickett.

General Robert E. Lee
I really have none to spare, but I am quite sure, besides, that they would prefer such a souvenir from one of the younger officers, and am confident that General Pickett would be pleased to give them one of his curls.

Lieutenant Frank Dawson, Confederate Army
General Pickett did not enjoy the joke, for he was known everywhere for his corkscrew ringlets, which were not particularly becoming when the rain made them lank in such weather as we then had.

Pickett was described as almost "womanly."

Captain Edward Baird, Pickett's staff officer
Brilliant in his strategy. He had the courage of a man with the tenderness of a woman.

Charles Pickett, George's brother
He was tender as he was brave.

Sallie, who became his wife four months after the Battle of Gettysburg, said of her husband:

Sallie Pickett
He sat on his horse with the grace of one who rides to win a [prize] from the hand of beauty rather than to meet the foe in deadly conflict. His face was almost womanly fair, and his soft, dark hair swept backward in the morning wind. Were ever grace and delicacy so opposed to the rude idea of war as in his person and life history?

Just about anywhere, everybody remembered George Pickett. A stunning description came from a Yankee prisoner of war, Bernhard Domschcke, who saw Pickett ride by on the morning of Pickett's Charge.

Captain Bernhard Domschcke
The archetype of a Virginia slave-baron strutted briskly, proud in bearing, head lifted in arrogance. On horseback, he looked like the ruler of a continent. Obviously, he took pains with his appearance, riding boots aglitter, near shoulder length hair tonsorially styled—but the color of his nose and upper cheeks betrayed that he pandered the inner man. Pleasures of the battle left indelible tracks. Indeed, the coarse plebian features in no way matched the efforts at aristocratic airs. He galloped proudly that morning from his tent to the front.

But would the flamboyant Pickett be able to force back the Federal lines? Would he be able to outflank Union General Alexander Hays? Would the remainder of the Union Army be neutralized before newly appointed Union commander George Meade figured out what Lee was trying to do and found a way to counter it?

Lee was absolutely certain the answer to all these questions was yes. The charge would scatter the entire Union Army, bring about victory, and set up the Southern forces for an uninterrupted march to Harrisburg and its large railroad depot. The Confederate Army would seize the trains there and have the engineers take them to Philadelphia in just a few hours. A stunned city, suddenly overrun with Confederates, would surrender. That would end the war.

If it did not, the Southerners could continue on the train line to New York City and end the war there. This one morning—July 3—could change the course of American history, and Lee completely understood that.

There were things that Pickett and Lee did not know. Exactly how many men did the Union have on top of Cemetery Ridge? And where were they positioned? How many cannon did they have left? How many were operational? The remaining strength of Meade's army was still an unanswered question.

General Pickett had just arrived at Gettysburg, but a long look around told him all he needed to know about what was going on. Thousands had been killed and tens of thousands had been wounded. Blood was everywhere. There had been a constant booming of cannon and the incessant sound of rifles and pistols for days.

On the morning of Pickett's Charge, soldiers on both sides took time to revel in the brief calm and marvel at the beauty of the small village of Gettysburg and the surrounding country dotted with tiny lanes and large farmlands. Thomas Galway, a Union officer from Cleveland in the 8th Ohio Infantry, who had immigrated to the United States from Ireland just twelve years earlier, was on Cemetery Ridge, about three hundred yards from Cemetery Hill on the early morning of Pickett's Charge. He was stunned by the beauty of the landscape.

....

Corporal Thomas Galway, Union Army

It is a pretty sight. We can see for miles around to the right and to the left. Way to the west are South Mountains, beyond which is Chambersburg. At our feet is a pretty valley about two miles wide, bounded on the far side by a low wooded ridge where we can plainly [see] the enemy's line. In the middle of the valley to our right lies the pleasant town of Gettysburg. . . .

In the middle of the night before Pickett's Charge, at about 1:00 A.M. in this Garden of Eden, hours before the bloodiest battle in American history to that point, Galway lifted his eyes to the heavens and saw another sensational sight—early, bright Union artillery fire.

Corporal Thomas Galway

As we lay on our backs courting sleep, we could at any time see the skies crossed with a network of the fiery traces of shells going and coming, like shooting stars, between the artillery of both sides. Shortly afterwards it became quiet, terrifically so considering the storm which we all knew had been brewing for the morrow.

Many things went wrong that day. The Southerners were unable to take nearby Culp's Hill and, consequently, the units pinned down there could not aid Pickett in his attack. Cavalry commander J. E. B. Stuart was ordered to attack the Union from the rear and scatter them. He was unable to do so.

The July 3 charge came to be known as Pickett's Charge because Pickett commanded three of the eleven Southern brigades in the attack, but the other eight were commanded by Generals James Pettigrew and Isaac Trimble, and all were under the command of a very nervous General Longstreet, who did not like the plan at all.

The charge itself, up Cemetery Hill, although well planned, started to misfire in the early morning. There were nothing but delays. Brigades could not be assembled quickly enough. Orders were sent slowly. Lee wanted the charge to get underway shortly after 8:00 A.M., when it was not too hot. But it did not get started until seven hours later, at 3:00 P.M., the absolute hottest hour of the day. It was 87°F and very humid when the attack finally began. The Confederates, who had to wait in the heat and scorching sun all day, were dehydrated and tired by then.

The Union troops simply watched and waited.

Union officer

The silence and the heat were oppressive. The troops stretched upon the ground with the hot July sun pouring upon them. . . . Some sat with haversacks on the knee, pencil in hand, writing to dear ones at home.

The charge did not get underway at 8:00 A.M. because no one was ready. Lee, frustrated, rode through the wood and along his lines at the appointed hour and did not see any of Pickett's men, who were supposed to have arrived the night before. No one else was ready to go, either. Lee finally found General Longstreet, who, it turned out, was responsible for holding back the charge all morning in order to change Lee's mind about it. Longstreet just could not order a charge he felt would be a catastrophe. It was another sign of the tension between the two Southern generals.

Longstreet told Lee that his men were not ready because he had scouts patrolling the entire Gettysburg area the previous night and was unable to get his men together for the assault.

General James Longstreet

General, I have had my scouts out all night and I find that you still have an excellent opportunity to move around to the right of Meade's army and maneuver him into attacking us.

Longstreet promised 10:00 A.M., and then 1:00 P.M., and then, finally, 3:00 P.M. The long delay should not have surprised Lee. On the previous day, Longstreet had been ordered to start an assault in the early morning, but it did not get underway until 4:00 P.M. because he disagreed with Lee's plans. Today again, Longstreet's foot-dragging was part of his overall effort to halt Pickett's Charge. Lee would have none of it.

Lee had listened to Longstreet's plan several times and believed he was dead wrong. There was no time for any more delays. Now, hearing it once more, and angry about yet another long delay in an attack plan, Lee shook his head and told Longstreet to order Pickett's Charge to move forward as quickly as possible.

Longstreet was furious with Lee's decision. He wrote after the war:

General James Longstreet

That he [Lee] was excited and off his balance was evident on the afternoon of [July 1], and he labored under that oppression until enough blood was shed to appease him.

Lee's supporters were angered by Longstreet's remarks. After the war, many Southerners claimed Longstreet and his delays were the reason the charge failed—and that the South lost the battle and the war.

Longstreet was not the only reason for the delay, though. Generals under him were not in position that hot morning. General Joseph Johnston had been caught up in an early morning battle with the Federals that never should have taken place—because by that time Longstreet was supposed to have led Pickett's Charge. By 3:00 P.M. Johnston and his men were exhausted and unable to join Pickett and his troops. General Ewell also could not join the attack because he had assumed it would begin at 8:00 A.M., and was now pinned down at Culp's Hill.

Lee apparently did not realize that. In his mind, Lee envisioned a smooth assault up Cemetery Hill to victory. He never took into consideration all the things that were going wrong, the strength of the enemy, or the reaction of General Meade.

There was also confusion on the part of Colonel E. Porter Alexander, Lee's chief artillery officer, who simply did not know what to do or when to do it. Southern firepower on the Union lines was badly aimed. Many shells did not explode or flew far over their intended targets.

Colonel Alexander, age twenty-eight, was a rising star in the Confederate Army. He had quickly moved up the ranks to colonel and was one of the heroes of the Battle of Fredericksburg when he mowed down federal troops there with his artillery.

He, like Longstreet, was not so sure that Lee was right about Pickett's Charge. There were tens of thousands of Union soldiers on top of that ridge and barely 12,500 men under Pickett going up a steep hill with little or no protection. Was it a brilliant, well-planned, calculated move by a great commander, or a reckless, let's-try-anything stab at the Federals by an angry commander who had been losing the battle for two days?

Colonel E. Porter Alexander, after getting Lee's attack order
I accordingly took position, about 12, at the most favorable point . . . with one of Pickett's couriers with me. Soon afterwards, I received the following note from [General] Longstreet: "Colonel: If the artillery fire does not have the effect to drive off the enemy or greatly demoralize him as to make our efforts pretty certain, I should prefer that you do not advise General Pickett to make the charge. I shall rely a great deal on your good judgment to determine the matter."

Alexander shook his head and reread Longstreet's note.

Colonel E. Porter Alexander
This note rather startled me. If that assault was to be made on General Lee's judgment it was all right. But I did not want it made on mine. I wrote back to General Longstreet to the following effect: "General: I will only be able to judge on the effect of our fire on the enemy by his return fire,

for his infantry is but little exposed to view and the smoke will obscure the whole field. If, as I infer from your note, there is any alternative to this attack, it should be carefully considered before opening our fire, for it will take all the artillery ammunition we have left to test this one thoroughly, and, if the result is unfavorable, we will have none left for another effort. And even if this is entirely successful, it can only be so at a very bloody cost."

General James Longstreet

I rode to a woodlands hard by, to lie down and study for some new thought that might aid the assaulting column. In a few minutes, report came from Alexander that he would only be able to judge of the effect of his fire by the return of the enemy, as his infantry was not exposed to view, and the smoke of the batteries would soon cover the field. He asked if there was an alternative, that it be carefully considered before the batteries opened, as there was not enough artillery and munitions for this.

Col. Alexander was informed that there was no alternative; that I could find no way out of it; that General Lee considered and would listen to nothing else; that orders had gone for the guns to give signal for the batteries; that he should call the troops at the first opportunity or lull in the enemy's fire.

And so Alexander waited and waited and waited for word from Longstreet.

At the same time that Alexander waited, so did everybody else on the Confederate line. The orders were for the Southerners to attack in Pickett's Charge, but ONLY after Longstreet had two guns fired as signals.

Shortly before 3:00 P.M., Lee, with Longstreet, rode all along the Confederate line that would soon make up Pickett's Charge, again targeting a clump of trees on top of the hill on Cemetery Ridge as the point where Trimble, Pettigrew, and Pickett would take their men. As Lee rode along the line, all his troops apparently supported his decision to go ahead with Pickett's Charge.

Reporter, *London Times*

A cry for immediate battle swelled the gale—timid and hesitating counsels were impatiently discarded . . . and the mature and cautious wisdom of General Lee had no choice but to float with the current and to trust the enthusiasm of his troops to carry him triumphantly . . . over the heights.

Lee's men would follow him anywhere, but that morning, looking up at that long hill in front of them, with an unknown number of cannons and Union soldiers at the top of it, some were nervous.

Nineteen-year-old Confederate lieutenant John Dooley, from Richmond, in the First Virginia Infantry, had been wounded at Chancellorsville. Now he suffered a twinge of anxiety as his regiment marched past General Lee, who was sitting on his horse watching the beginning of the charge.

Lieutenant John Dooley, Confederate Army

As we pass him [Lee], the admiring throngs doff their warworn hats and greet his presence with reiterated shouts and most enthusiastic waves.

Dooley, though, ignoring the cheering, looked at Lee's face and was worried.

Lieutenant John Dooley

I must confess that the Gen'ls face does not look as bright as [when] he were certain of success. But yet it is impossible for us to be otherwise than victorious and we press forward with beating hearts.

Dooley and his fellow Confederates moved on and joined the long, long line of men and cannon that prepared for the charge. He saw the movement of different batteries of cannon around him and, in the distance, heard the rumble of hundreds of horses in the Confederate cavalry as they moved into position elsewhere. Time drifted by ever so slowly.

Orders came that Dooley and his men were to charge at a signal from Longstreet's cannon. They were to go up the hill and head for a clump of trees, visible to all, on the top of it. All of the 12,000+ men were to converge there and crash through the Union line. At the same time, General Stuart's cavalry would attack the Federals from the rear.

Dooley and his men were early targets of the pre-charge cannon duel between North and South, and shells exploded all around them.

Lieutenant John Dooley

In one of our reg'ts alone, the killed and wounded, even before going into the charge, amounted to 88 men, and men lay bleeding and gasping in the agonies of death all around and we are unable to help them in the least. . . . Some companion would raise his head disfigured and unrecognizable, streaming with blood, or would stretch his full length, his limbs quivering in the pangs of death.

Confederate officer

I look around [and] what a change, from order to chaos, from beauty to destruction, from life to death—levelled fences, splintered trees, furrowed ground, broken cannon, exploded caissons, slaughtered horses, mangled men.

Seventeen-year-old Union corporal Thomas Galway's regiment of the 8th Ohio Volunteer Infantry had moved to a spot near the Emmitsburg Road and waited for whatever action the Confederate Army would take. They were under fire when they were seen moving as part of the pre-charge skirmish.

Corporal Thomas Galway, Union Army

All this drew a brisk fire from the enemy, which continued ceaselessly from then out. The rails of the fence had been torn away from the posts and laid upon one another, making a sort of protection for the heads of the men lying down behind them. Well, when we reached the fence, we saw what work Death had done. . . . Our dead lay so thick where they had been killed that it was difficult for us to find a place to stretch ourselves.

It was now early afternoon and hot. Galway was surprised to see a Rebel soldier drop down from a tree some thirty yards away.

Confederate soldier

Don't fire, Yanks!

Corporal Thomas Galway

We all got up to see who was coming.

A man with his gun slung over his shoulder came [over] from the tree. Several of our fellows aimed at him but the others checked them, to see what would follow. The man had a canteen in his hand and, when he had come half-way to us we saw him [God bless him] kneel down and give a drink to one of our wounded, who lay there beyond us. Of course, we cheered the reb, and heard someone shouted, "bully for you, Johnny!" Whilst this had been going on, we had all risen to our feet. The enemy, too, having ceased to fire, were also standing. As soon as the sharpshooter had finished his generous work, he turned around and went back to the tree, and then at the top of his voice, shouted "down yanks, we're going to fire!" And down we lay again and the shooting in the pre-charge skirmish resumed.

Finally, at 3:00 P.M. . . .

General James Longstreet

The signal guns broke the silence, the blaze of the second gun mingling in the smoke of the first, and salvos rolled to the left and repeating themselves along the ridges, the enemy's fine metal spreading its fire to the converging lines of the Confederates, plowing the trembling ground, plunging through the line of batteries and clouding the heavy air. Two or three hundred guns seemed proud of their undivided honors of organized confusion. The Confederates had the benefit of converging fire into the enemy's massed position, but the superior metal of the enemy neutralized the advantages of position. The brave and steady work progressed.

Although he did not approve of the charge, General Longstreet helped lead it, and in grand fashion.

General James Kemper, Pickett's aide

Longstreet rode slowly and alone, immediately in front of our entire line. He sat on his large charger with a magnificent grace and composure I never before beheld. His bearing was to me the grandest mortal spectacle of the war. I expected to see him fall every instant. Still, he moved on, slowly and majestically, with an inspiring confidence, composure, self-possession, and repressed power in every movement and look that fascinated me.

General James Longstreet

[I] am greatly distressed at this, but let us hold our ground awhile longer. We are hurting the enemy badly, and will charge him presently.

Lieutenant George Finley, 56th Virginia, Confederate Army

[I saw Longstreet] riding slowly from our right in front of our line and in full view of the enemy skirmishers. [Longstreet] did not seem to notice

the enemy skirmishers but was cooly and carefully inspecting ours; [we expected him to be hit at any moment]. As rifle balls whistled by and a shell now and then ploughed up the ground close to and startled the splendid horse he rode, the general would check him and quietly ride on.

Captain John Holmes Smith, Confederate Army

Just before the artillery fire ceased, General Longstreet rode in a walk between the artillery and the infantry, in front of the regiment toward the left and disappeared down the line. He was as quiet as an old farmer riding over his plantation on a Sunday morning, and looked neither to the right or left.

It had been known for hours that we were to assail the enemy's lines in front. We fully expected to take them.

Men along the line shouted to Longstreet to go to the rear. One yelled:

Confederate soldier

You'll get your old fool head knocked off.

Just before the artillery barrage ended, Longstreet dashed off a quick note and sent it to Colonel E. Porter Alexander.

General James Longstreet

Colonel: The intention is to advance the infantry if the artillery has the desired effect of driving the enemy off, or to have other effect, such as to warrant us to join, making the attack. When the moment arrives, advise General Pickett and of course advance such artillery as you can [to move the troops forward].

A note arrived from General Ambrose Wright, who had been wounded earlier at Chancellorsville. Wright and his men had taken a part of the key Cemetery Ridge on July 2, but were forced out by larger Union forces.

General Ambrose Wright, Confederate Army
It is not so hard to go there [the top of Cemetery Ridge] as it looks. I was nearly there with my brigade yesterday. The trouble is to stay there. The whole Yankee army is there in a bunch.

All the decisions being made by Alexander, Pickett, and Longstreet were done amid the boom of gunfire on both sides that was taking its toll. Furthermore, Colonel Alexander was influenced by a rumor wildly circulated in camp a few hours earlier that General Lee was going to send "every man he could" along with General Pickett, tens of thousands of them, and would need heavy artillery support.

Colonel E. Porter Alexander
I rode to see Pickett, who was with his divisions a short distance in the rear. I did not tell him my object, but only trying to guess how he felt about the charge. He seemed very sanguine and thought himself in luck to have the chance. Then I felt I could not make any delay or let the attack suffer by any indecision on our part, and that General Longstreet might know of my intention, I wrote him only this: "General: When our artillery fire is at its best I shall order Pickett to charge."

Union Corporal Thomas Galway and his regiment had moved to a position near the Emmitsburg Road.

Corporal Thomas Galway
All this drew a brisk fire from the enemy.

Colonel E. Porter Alexander

It was one o'clock in the afternoon when the battlefield's quiet was rudely broken by the boom of Longstreet's signal guns. Within moments, every soldier in Meade's lines knew that a titanic move was afoot.

Union Major St. Clair Mulholland, who had been awarded the Medal of Honor for bravery at Chancellorsville, was positioned with Hancock's 2nd Corps just south of Cemetery Hill and in a perfect position to witness the enormous surge of men.

Major St. Clair Mulholland

The headquarters wagons had just come up and General George Gibbons had invited Hancock and the staff to partake of some lunch. The bread that was handed around—and it WAS eaten—was consumed without butter for, as the orderly was passing the latter article to the gentlemen, a shell from Seminary Ridge cut him in two. Instantly, the air was filled with bursting shells. The whole hundred and thirty seven guns which now began to play upon us seemed to be discharged simultaneously, as if [by] electricity.

The big battle everyone had anticipated on the third day was ready to start. Yet Pickett's infantry was not moving as Lee had ordered.

Colonel E. Porter Alexander

I [wanted to] order [an] advance within ten or twenty minutes. But when I looked at the full development of the enemy's batteries, and knew that his infantry was generally protected from our fire by stone walls and swells of ground, I could not bring myself to give the word. It seemed madness to launch infantry into that fire, with nearly three-quarters of a mile to go at midday under a July sun. I waited 25 minutes hoping vainly for something to turn up.

Alexander really did not know what to do. He quickly sent a note to General Pickett.

Colonel E. Porter Alexander
If you are coming [forward] at all, you just come at once, or I cannot give you proper support; but the enemy's fire has not slackened at all; at least 18 guns are firing from the cemetery itself.

The Union guns then went quiet and the guns in the cemetery were rolled away. Lee seemed to be right about a mass Union retreat. Alexander hoped so.

Colonel E. Porter Alexander, to an aide
If the [Union] does not run fresh batteries in there in five minutes, this is our fight. I looked anxiously with my glass and the five minutes passed without a sign of life on the deserted position still swept by our fire, and littered with dead men and horses and fragments of disabled carriages.

What Alexander did not know was that Brigadier General Henry Hunt, head of the Union artillery, had been given enormous leeway by Meade in decision-making—something that he did not have under Hooker. Hunt had ordered his men to stop firing to trick Lee and Alexander into thinking he was out of ammunition—which he was not. Unknown to Hunt, his actions also caused Lee to believe that his own cannon fire had destroyed most of the North's cannon, which it had not.

General Henry Hunt, Union Army
I now rode along the ridge to inspect the [area's] batteries. The infantry were lying down in its reverse slope, near the crest, in open ranks, waiting events. As I passed along, a bolt from a rifle-gun struck the ground just in

front of a man of the front rank, penetrated the surface and passed under him, throwing him "over and over." He fell behind there . . . apparently dead, and a ridge of earth where he had been lying reminded me of the backwoods practice of "barking" squirrels.

Our fire was deliberate, but on inspecting the [ammunition] chests, I found that the ammunition was running low, and hastened to General Meade to advise its immediate cessation and preparation for the assault which would certainly follow. The headquarters building, immediately behind the ridge, had been abandoned, and many of the horses of the staff lay dead. Being told that the general [Meade] had gone to the cemetery, I proceeded thither. He was not there, and on telling General Howard my object, he concurred in its propriety and I rode back along the ridge, ordering the fire to cease. This was followed by a cessation of that of the enemy, under the mistaken impression that he had silenced our guns, and almost immediately his infantry came out of the woods for assault [thinking there would be little firing upon them].

Shortly after that, several Confederates heard that Meade, in an effort to save ammunition because he had so little, had ordered his batteries to stop firing. This confirmed Alexander's faith in Lee's decision, which he had made based upon misinformation and gross misjudgments.

The great Union ruse had worked.

Alexander hastily scribbled another note to Pickett.

Colonel E. Porter Alexander

For God's sake, come quick. The 18 guns are gone and my ammunition won't let me support you properly.

Pickett, on a horse next to General Longstreet, was handed Alexander's note as he started to write a letter to his girlfriend, Sallie, whom he called "Sallie of the sweet eyes."

General George Pickett

After reading [Alexander's note] I handed it to [Longstreet] and asked if I should obey and go forward. He looked at me for a moment and then held out his hand [to shake mine] and bowed his head on his breast. I shall never forget the look in his face or the clasp of his hand.

General James Longstreet

The order was imperative. The Confederate commander [Lee] had fixed his heart upon the work. Just then, a number of the enemy's batteries hitched up and hauled off, which gave a glimpse of unexpected hope. Encouraging messages were sent for the columns to hurry on, and they were then on [an] elastic springing step. General Pickett, a graceful horseman, sat lightly in the saddle, his brown locks flowing quite over his shoulders. Pettigrew's division spread their steps and quickly rectified the alignment, and the grand march moved bravely on. General Trimble mounted, adjusting his seat and reins as if setting out on a pleasant afternoon ride. When aligned to their places, a solid march was made down the slope and past our batteries in position.

General George Pickett

Then, General, I shall lead my division on.

Pickett rode away, stopped, and then went back to Longstreet.

General George Pickett, thinking of his Sallie

I asked the dear old chief if he would be good enough to mail this letter to you [if I died in the charge]. . . . As he took the letter from me, my darling, I saw tears glistening on his cheeks and beard. The stern old war horse, God bless him, was for his men and, I know, praying, too, that his cup might pass from them.

Longstreet turned as Pickett went to take charge of his men for the assault, and rode to where he knew Colonel Alexander was. Longstreet did not want to countermand Lee's attack order, but still tried to sabotage it indirectly with Alexander. Longstreet had told Lee, very bluntly, that Pickett's Charge would fail.

General James Longstreet, to Lee

General, I have been a soldier all my life. I have been with soldiers engaged in fights by couples, by squads, companies, regiments, divisions, and armies, and should know, as well as anyone, what soldiers can do. It is my opinion that no fifteen thousand men ever arrayed for battle can take that position.

General James Longstreet, to Alexander

Stop Pickett immediately and replenish your ammunition.

Colonel E. Porter Alexander

I explained to him that it would take too long and that the enemy would recover from the effect our fire was then having and that we had, moreover, very little to replenish with.

General James Longstreet

I don't want to make this attack. I would stop it now but that General Lee ordered it and expects it to go on. I don't see how it can succeed.

Colonel E. Porter Alexander

I listened, but did not dare offer a word. The battle was lost if we stopped. Ammunition was far too low to try anything else, for we had been fighting three days. While Longstreet was still weeping, Pickett's division had swept out of the woods and showed the full length of its gray ranks and shining bayonets, as grand a sight as ever a man looked on. Looking on the left, Pettigrew stretched farther than I could see. General Dick Garnett, just out of the sick ambulance, and buttoned up in an old blue overcoat, riding at the head of his brigade, passed us and saluted Longstreet. . . . I rode with him a short distance, and then we wished each other luck and a good bye, which was our last.

The Confederate force was 12,500 or so strong. They were observed by many, and all the observers wondered whether Pickett would charge and if he would succeed. The attack he and his men were about to make would take them three-quarters of a mile up a hill all without any protection at all—except one another. If Lee was right about the Federals' artillery, the Rebels would reach the top, destroy the Union Army, and win the war. If he was wrong, they would be blown to pieces.

Pickett, on his horse Old Black, rode up in front of his men and made a short, heartfelt, impassioned speech.

General George Pickett
Up men, and to your posts! Don't forget today that you are from Old Virginia!

Finally, around 3:00 P.M., the charge started. Sometimes quickly and sometimes slowly, regiments large and small emerged from the woods and headed up the hill. It was not a "charge," but a slowly moving assault, Pettigrew and Trimble and their men were on the left and Pickett on the right. Up and down the lines, officers shouted "March!" or "Forward" and, stepping briskly, 12,500 men began the attack up that steep hill and into rifle and pistol fire.

The men marched slowly and deliberately and did not actually "charge" until they were near the top of the hill. The nine brigades stretched nearly a mile across the field. They had not gone very far when the Union artillery, dormant for so long, opened up on them—to

Lee's great surprise. They were hit by the full force of the eighty-seven cannon on top of the hill and also by the hidden batteries of Lieutenant Colonel Freeman McGilvery's men north of Little Round Top, who raked the Southerners' right flank. Cannons from Cemetery Hill fired on them from the left. At the center of the hill II Corps blasted away.

The damage to the marching Southern troops was considerable, and right away men fell and died—in clumps, in pairs, and standing alone. When the Confederates came within some four hundred yards of the top of the hill, the Federals opened up with more canister and musket fire.

Onlookers had an uninterrupted view of perhaps the single greatest moment of the Civil War.

A reporter for the *Richmond Enquirer* witnessed the charge from start to finish and shook his head as it began.

Reporter, *Richmond Enquirer*
I stood upon an eminence and watched this advance with great interest. I had seen brave men [Confederate general Wright's brigade] pass over that fated valley the day before. I had witnessed their death struggle with the foe on the opposite heights. I had watched their return with shattered ranks, a bleeding mass, but with sustained banners. Now, I saw their valiant comrades prepare for the same bloody trial, and already felt that their efforts would be vain unless their supports should be as true as steel and brave as lions.

Union soldier Jesse Bowman Young viewed the scene from the other side of Cemetery Ridge.

Lieutenant Jesse Bowman Young, Union Army
Standing on the hill where the Union troops are posted, let us try to picture that almost matchless moment. A stone fence is almost immediately to our front with batteries of artillery lining the slope. Look about you:

here are bronzed and worn veterans in blue with a set and dogged expression on their lips and in their eyes, line after line of them massed on both slopes [of Cemetery Ridge] and on the crest of the ridge in support of the batteries. In front, towards the west, is the advanced line of Union troops [skirmishers] and beyond them are pleasant fields rolling in beauty. The fences are mostly broken down. . . .

Over this plain and over these batteries and upon this stone wall, more than 10,000 men are about to be led with a furious and indomitable courage not to be paralleled by any other martial achievement hitherto wrought by the Army of Northern Virginia. As we look with bated breath and quivering nerves on the landscape, we behold the shimmer of steel along the distant ridge, and then the flutter of banners, and then an advancing line of men.

Major Edmund Rice, Union Army

A line of Confederate skirmishers sprang slightly forward . . . and, with intervals well kept, moved rapidly down into the open fields, closely followed by a line of battle, and then by another, and then by a third, almost a mile in length. Both sides watched this never to be forgotten scene, the grandeur of attack by so many thousands of men. Gibbons's division, which was to stand the brunt of the assault, looked with admiration upon the different lines of Confederates marching forward with easy swinging step, and our men were heard to exclaim, "Here they come!"

Also watching the start of the charge was Union General Carl Schurz.

General Carl Schurz, Union Army

The [Southern] alignment was perfect. The battle flags fluttered gaily over the bayonets, glittering in the sunlight. . . . Through our field glasses we could distinctly see the gaps torn in their ranks and the ground dotted with dark spots of their dead and wounded. Now and then a cheer went up from our lines when our men observed some of our shells striking right among the advancing enemy and scattering death and destruction around. But the brave rebels promptly filled the gaps from behind or by closing up on their colors; and unshaken and unhesitating they continued their onward. . . . So far not a musket had been discharged from behind the stone fence protecting our regiment.

Up on top of Cemetery Ridge, General Gibbon, field glasses in hand, peered down at the Confederates as they started their charge.

General John Gibbon, Union Army

. . . A magnificent sight met my eyes. The enemy in a long gray line was marching towards us over the rolling ground in our front. Their flags fluttering in the air and serving as guides to their line of battle.

"Here they come! Here they come!" shouted dozens of Union soldiers as the gray line moved up the field.

Union soldier from New Jersey

[It was] the grandest sight I have ever seen. Their lines looking to be as straight as a line could be, their bayonets glistening in the sun, from right to left as far as the eye could see.

Colonel E. Porter Alexander, Confederate Army

As our supporting guns advanced, we passed many poor, mangled victims left in [our] trampled wake . . . one with the most horrible wound that I ever saw. We were halted for a moment by a fence, and as the men threw it down for the guns to pass, I saw in one of the corners a man sitting down and looking up at me. A solid shot had carried away both jaws and his tongue. I noticed the powder smut from the shot on the white skin around the wound. He sat up and looked at me steadily and I looked at him until the guns could pass, but nothing, of course, could be done for him.

The beginning of the charge was witnessed by Abner Small of the 16th Maine, who, with his comrades, had waited most of the day for it to start. Then, sometime around three, it did.

Lieutenant Abner Small, Union soldier

Away down the Emmitsburg Road a rebel cannon flashed, and a puff of smoke blew and hung on the still summer air; then another, then from all the rebel line there was one vast roar, and a storm of screaming metal swept across the valley. Our guns blazed and thundered in reply. The earth groaned and trembled. The air, thick with smoke and sulphurous vapor, almost suffocated the troops in support of the batteries. Through the murk we heard hoarse commands, the bursting of shells, cries of agony. We saw caissons hit and blown up, splinters flying, men flung to the ground, horses torn and shrieking. Solid shot hit the hill in our front, sprayed battalions with fountains of dirt, and went plunging into the ranks, crushing flesh and bone. Under that awful sight, continuous, relentless, our brigade and all our line held tight and unfaltering.

About two o'clock our brigade was moved from the left to the right of the cemetery and placed in support of batteries there. How that short move was made I don't know. The air was murderous iron; it seemed there could not be room for any soldier upright and in motion. We stayed an hour in our new position, exposed not only to shelling from east and west, but also to the galling fire of rebel skirmishers. . . .

About three o'clock we were again moved to the left, from the hill to the ridge. Many of the Union guns were now ceasing their fire, damaged batteries were going to the rear, and others were hurrying up from the reserve. Shot and shell from the enemy still pounded the hill. The ground was strewn with dead horses. Here and there were dead men. We wondered, as we passed through the cemetery, that we weren't smashed into the earth with moldering citizens of peace.

There was a dull roar in the air as the 12,500 Southern soldiers continued their march toward Cemetery Ridge and the Union troops on top of it, who greatly outnumbered them—although the Rebels did not know that. There was sporadic fire at this point and the sound of some far-off cannon down at the woodlands near the bottom of the hill. There were muffled shouts of encouragement from both North and South. You could hear the trudging of men's boots, some rustle of rifles being taken down from shoulders, the far-off wheels of cannon.

Corporal Galway's regiment had moved and was now about to take the brunt of the charge. He was stunned by it.

Corporal Thomas Galway, Union Army
I had often read of battles and of charges, but until this moment I had not gazed upon so grand a sight as was presented by that beautiful mass of gray, as it came on, cheering their peculiar cheer, right towards the crest of the hill, which we and our batteries were to defend.

Lieutenant Dooley, on the Confederate side, felt stunned in a different way.

Lieutenant John Dooley, Confederate Army
I tell you, there is no romance in making one of these charges. When you rise to your feet, I tell you the enthusiasm of ardent breasts in many cases ain't there. Instead of a burning [desire] to avenge the insults of our country, families, and altars and firesides, the thought is mostly frequently, oh, if I could just come out of this charge safely, how thankful would I be.

The sound of cannon and muskets and pistols was everywhere, thumping endlessly in the ears of all.

Lieutenant Abner Small, Union Army
As we hastened towards the ridge, we heard a thunder of artillery there, and musketry that wasn't the crash of volley or the harsh rattle of scattered

firing, but one continuous din. The long-awaited assault had come. As we topped the ridge, we caught another sound of the uproar, strange and terrible; a sound that came from thousands of human throats, yet was not a comingling of shouts and yells, but rather like a vast mournful roar.

The gray horses swept toward the side of Galway's regiment, which kept firing at the enemy. And, of course, there was the ceaseless, noisy sound of that famous, high-pitched, shrieking Rebel yell.

Corporal Thomas Galway
We now heard the fearful din of our artillery, the savage, threatening yells of the advancing and now seemingly invincible enemy. . . . We stood all alone out in the open field.

For some reason, the Confederate line never attacked Galway's company, although it would have been easy enough to overrun.

Corporal Thomas Galway
The enemy column has now approached the turnpike just to the South of us. . . . Still brave and cheering, they ascend the stone wall. Our men up there break and disappear beyond the crest of the ridge [and] for a few seconds things look dubious. The enemy has taken Griffin's battery and are about to train its guns on our own line.

The charge was at full throttle and Dooley found himself close to the top of the hill.

Lieutenant John Dooley
Thirty more yards and the guns are ours.

The fire was intense.

Lieutenant John Dooley

Who can stand such a storm of hissing lead and iron? Our men are falling faster now, for the deadly musket is at work. Volley after volley of crashing musket balls swept through the line and mowed us down like wheat before the scythe.

Dooley got to the top of the hill and then was hit by musket balls. He looked down and saw the blood spurting from his legs.

Lieutenant John Dooley

Shot through both thighs, I fall about thirty yards from the guns. By my side lies Lt. Kehoe, shot through the knee. . . . Here we lie, he in excessive pain, I fearing to bleed to death, the dead and dying all around, while the division sweeps over the Yankee guns. . . . We seem to have victory in our hands.

In that brief moment Dooley thought he saw hundreds of Confederate troops coming to the aid of his regiment and about to take the hill. He was confused; they were Union troops. They were shooting down the Southerners and firing away at them with large artillery batteries.

Dooley was captured and spent twenty months in a Union prisoner of war camp.

The Confederates began moving back down the hill in retreat, faster and faster. Galway, just below the ridge, recorded the action.

Corporal Thomas Galway, Union Army

A major sorty, . . . rallying a portion of the 29th New York, charges them and recovers the battery. The enemy, now broken and disorganized and far from support, begin to retire. The retreat is almost at once turned into a flight! [They] throw away everything—cartridge boxes, waistbelts, and haversacks—in their stampede. As far as the eye could reach, the ground was covered with flying Confederates.

Arthur Fremantle, British journalist
[The valley before Cemetery Ridge] was covered by Confederates slowly and sulkily returning toward us in small, broken parties under heavy artillery fire.

General Longstreet watched the retreat with sadness, but exhibited a toughness at the same time.

Arthur Fremantle, British journalist
No person could have been more calm or self-possessed than General Longstreet. . . . I could now thoroughly appreciate the term "bulldog" which I had heard applied to him by the soldiers.

Union Captain Winfield Scott summed up the view of the Pickett catastrophe from the Federal side better than most.

Captain Winfield Scott, Union Army
From our position, we could overlook that whole ball between the two lines. . . . All at once, over their works and through the bushes that skirted them, came a heavy skirmish line. The skirmishers were about two spaces apart, covering about three-quarters of a mile of our front. Behind them about 20 rods came another heavy skirmish line. Behind them, about the same distance, came out the first line of battle. As they first emerged, had they continued straight to the front, their charge would have been centered upon the troops to our left.

It was a magnificent line of battle. Over three-quarters of a mile long. The men carried their guns, with bayonets fixed at right shoulder. The regimental flags and guidons were plainly visible along the whole line.

The guns and bayonets in the sunlight shone like silver. The whole line of battle looked like a stream or river of silver moving towards us. Behind this came the regimental officers; while behind them mounted and followed by their aides, came the brigade and division commanders, with their orderlies carrying their guidons and headquarters flags.

Then came the second line of infantry, in the same form and order as the first, followed by their commanders on horses. Behind this still, in heavy massed columns on the center and wings, were the supports and reserves. Two streaming lines of silver led off, decorated and livened by their battle flags. Their order was magnificent. The movement of such a force over such a field, in such perfect order, to such a destiny, was grand beyond expression. After moving forward about a quarter of a mile, a change was made in the direction of the line. A left half wheel was executed and they came straight for us, so that their left would just strike the right of our brigade. . . .

The whole line, to us who were in front, seemed straight as an arrow—the whole force like a perfect and magnificent parade. My own heart was thrilled at the sight. I was so absorbed with the beauty and grandeur of the scene that I became oblivious to the shells that were bursting about us. This passage of scripture came to my mind, and I repeated it aloud: "Fair as the moon, bright as the sun, and terrible as an army with banners."

Captain Scott prepared for a lethal barrage.

Captain Winfield Scott

Shortly their skirmishers came within range. Ours reserved their fire until the enemy came close to them. Our fire was then so accurate and severe, that their first line was held in check and could not force ours back. The second line of skirmishers reinforced the first, and ours then began to yield, falling back slowly. Our batteries from Cemetery Hill fired over our heads and threw shells, which went through the lines, bursting among them. Gaps were opened and quickly closed again. The shells kept flying, gaps opened and closed, and the silver lines in perfect order came on. Skirmishers fired sharply; the horsemen galloped to and fro behind the lines as the goal was approached. The half-wheel of the enemy exposed their flank to the fire of McGilvery's and Hazlett's guns from near Round Top. But there was no flinching. Gaps opened and closed, but the lines came forward.

As the lines neared us, the enemy's batteries slackened. Our batteries in the front line opened with grape and canister. Greater gaps were opened and quickly closed, and still on in sublime order came the silver lines. It was then cannon, and gaps and closing of ranks, and on, on, on, in magnificent and unflinching valor came the lines of silvery steel. . . . The commands and the tramp of the on-coming hosts could now be heard. There was a moment quiet of skirmishes and musketry. Orders of the enemy, a little clearer and sharper, ran out upon the air. Another crash of cannister—other and terrifying gaps, and still heroic closing of ranks. Our first line by the stone wall was held by troops of Webb's brigade. They clutched their muskets and fixed their bayonets. The order was given to hold their fire until the enemy was close upon them.

Lieutenant George Finley, Confederate Army

Where I marched through a wheat field that sloped gently towards the Emmitsburg Road, the position of the Federals flashed into view. Skirmishers lined the fences along the road, and in back of them, along a low stone wall, or fence, gleamed the muskets of the first line. In rear of this, artillery, thickly planted, frowned upon us.

As we came in sight, there seemed to be a restlessness and excitement along the enemy's lines, which encouraged some of us to hope they would not make a stubborn resistance. Their skirmishers began to run in and the artillery opened upon us all along our front. I soon noticed that shells were also coming from our right. I discovered that they came from . . . the Round Tops. This fire soon became strictly enfilading as we changed the point of direction . . . to the left while on the march, and whenever it struck our ranks it was fearfully destructive. Lone companies, a little to our right, numbering thirty-five or forty men, were almost swept, to a man, from the line by a single shell. We had not advanced far beyond our own guns when our gallant colonel [W. D.] Stuart, fell, mortally wounded . . . we had no other field officer present, and the command devolved upon the senior captain.

The entire area was caught up in cannon fire and troops marching up the hill toward the Union line. Colonel Alexander moved from one area of the field to another, checking his guns and determining which ones were ready to fire upon the Federals.

Colonel E. Porter Alexander, Confederate Army

I rode down the line of guns, selecting such as had enough ammunition to follow Pickett's advance, and starting them after him as fast as possible. I got, I think, fifteen or eighteen in all . . . and went with them . . . the eighteen [Federal] guns were back in the cemetery [adding to] the storm of shell . . . bursting over and among our infantry . . . All of our guns silent as the infantry passed between them—reopened over their heads when the lines had got a couple of hundred yards away, but the enemy's artillery let us alone and fired only at the infantry. No one could have looked at that advance without feeling proud of it.

Getting to the top of the hill was nearly impossible. The Confederates found a depression in the Emmitsburg Road that offered some shelter from the murderous cannon fire, and thousands of Confederates jammed themselves into it as the smoke gathered above them. They were issued orders to leave and advance up the hill. Many surrendered to the Federals who arrived. Roughly one-third of the Confederates did not make that last four hundred yards or so of the charge and either surrendered or fled back down the hill.

Lieutenant Abner Small, Union Army

Down the slope in front of us, the ground was strewn with soldiers in every conceivable vehemence of action and agony, and death. Men in grey, surrounded and overwhelmed, were throwing up their hands in surrender. Others were falling back into the valley. Many were lying in the trampled fields, dying and dead. The assault had failed. I felt pity for the victims of that ruined hope. Looking down on the scene of their defeat and of our victory, I could only see a square mile of [sadness].

The men of the 8th Ohio Infantry, about 160 of them, suddenly lined up in a long, single line and, taking deadly aim, began a fusillade of force, loading and reloading, with devastating effect. Hundreds of Confederates were in their sights, and those who were not hit retreated as quickly as they could back down the hill.

More than 1,600 rounds of bullets were fired at General's Pettigrew's men struggling to make it up the hill. Union troops, crouched behind a stone wall, began firing away at around 4:00 P.M. with deadly aim. They had four lines deep and each line reloaded and immediately replaced the men of the line that had just fired, creating an interminable succession of brutal rifle fire. The attacking Southerners were cut to pieces.

North Carolina brigades, headed by Colonel William Lowrance, had lost two-thirds of their men on July 1, and the rest were being mowed down. In the middle of the fight, Lowrance was wounded.

Confederate orders were confused, misread, or not delivered. General Trimble held some of his men back and ordered others up the hill, with no apparent reason.

On the Union side, the leadership of General Alexander Hays was inspiring. He rode back and forth among his troops, sword waving in the air, shouting, "We're giving them hell, boys." He never flinched as bullet after bullet whizzed past him. The fire directed at him was so intense that two of his horses were shot out from under him.

General Pickett and his men crossed the Emmitsburg Road, but as soon as they did they were hit by heavy fire from Lieutenant Colonel McGilvery's cannon. Here Union General Hancock, who had been riding back and forth to encourage his men for more than forty-five minutes, was shot in the thigh and started to bleed. He refused advice to withdraw to the rear and heroically continued to lead his men.

Most of Pickett's men were stopped at a low stone wall defended by General Alexander Webb's Philadelphia Brigade. Webb quickly wheeled two cannons from across the field to the front of his brigade and began firing, causing tremendous damage to the Rebel forces.

General Carl Schurz, Union Army

Holding a stone fence on the hill [Cemetery Ridge], [soldiers] opened a rapid fire upon us with muskets . . . Men were falling all around. . . . cannons and muskets were raining death upon us. Still on and up the slope towards that stone fence, our men steadily swept, without a sound or a shot, save as the men would clamor to be allowed to return the fire was being poured into them.

It was towards Union General Alexander Webb's brigade of Gibbon's division of Hancock's corps that the brunt of the Southern attack was pointed. Although reduced to a fraction of its original size, its flank supports fighting simply to survive [and a brigade of reinforcements from across the valley entering upon a similar plight], the spearhead retained an incredible sharpness. When we were about seventy-five or one hundred yards from that stone wall, some of the men holding it began to break for the rear when, without orders, save from captains and lieutenants, our line poured a volley or two into them, and then rushed upon the fence. . . . The Federal gunners stood manfully to their guns. [I] never saw more gallant bearing in any men. They fired their last shots full in our faces and so close that I thought I felt distinctly the flame of the explosion.

The entire charge had been organized chaos, with Pickett's men swept by fire from atop Cemetery Ridge. The pounding of the hundreds of cannons was horrific.

Colonel E. Porter Alexander, Confederate Army

Streams of screaming projectiles cut through the hot air, falling and bursting everywhere. Men and horses were torn limb from limb; caissons exploded one after another in rapid succession, blowing the gunners to pieces. No spot within our lines was free from this frightful iron rain . . . It was literally a storm of shot and shell that the oldest soldiers there—those who had taken part in almost every battle of the war—had not yet witnessed. The awful rushing sound of the flying missiles, which causes the firmest hearts to quail, was everywhere.

Bonaparte, a pseudonym for a reporter for the *New York World*, a reporter for the *New York World*, watched the charge from on top of Cemetery Hill.

Bonaparte, *New York World*

The storm broke upon us so suddenly that soldiers and officers—who leaped [up] from their tents and from lazy siestas on the grass—were stricken to their rising with mortal wounds, and died, some with cigars between their teeth, some with pieces of food in their fingers and one, at least, a pale young German from Pennsylvania, with a miniature [picture] of his sister in his hands . . . The boards of fences, scattered by explosion, flew in splinters through the air. The earth, torn up in clouds, blinded the eyes of hurrying men and through the branches of the trees and among the gravestones in the cemetery a shower of destruction crashed ceaseless. As with hundreds of others, I groped through this tempest of death for the shelter of a bluff. An old man, a private in a company belonging to the 24th Michigan, was struck scarcely ten feet away by a cannonball which tore through him, extorting such a low, intense cry of mortal pain as I pray God I may never again [hear].

Union Captain Samuel Fiske, an officer in General Hancock's Federal Corps, was moved by the irony of what he saw.

Captain Samuel Fiske, Union Army
It was touching to see the little birds all out of their wits with fright, flying wildly about midst the tornado of missiles and uttering strange notes of distress. It was touching to see the innocent cows and calves feeding in the fields, torn in pieces by the shell. . . . It was a nobler sight to see the sublime bravery of our gallant artillerists serving their guns with the utmost precision and coolness.

Meanwhile, General Meade's headquarters on Taneytown Road took a pounding by the Southern rows of cannon. Shells burst around it repeatedly. One of the reporters in Meade's office was Samuel Wilkeson, whose son Bayard had been killed in the battle just two days earlier, on July 1.

Samuel Wilkeson, reporter, *New York Times*
Every size and form . . . of British and American gunnery shrieked, whirled, moaned, whistled and wrathfully fluttered over our ground. As many as six in a second, constantly two in a second, burning and screaming over and around headquarters made a very hell of fire that amazed the oldest officers. They burst in the yard—burst next to the fence on both sides, garnished as usual with the hitched horses of aides and orderlies. The fastened animals reared and plunged with terror. Then one fell, then another. . . . Through the midst of the storm of screaming [and] exploding shells, and ambulances, driven by its frenzied conductors at full speed, presented to all of us the marvelous spectacle of a horse going rapidly on three legs. A hinder one had been shot off at the hock. A shell tore up the little step of the headquarters cottage, the Leister house, and ripped bags of oats as if with a knife. Another soon carried off one of its two porch pillars.

General Gibbon was one of the officers who had been invited to a lunch of stewed rooster and coffee at headquarters. He was shocked by the bombardment.

General John Gibbon, Union Army

How long we sat there it is impossible to say, but after a long silence along the line, a single gun was heard off in my front and everyone's attention was attracted . . . . [The] air above us and surrounding us was filled with bursting and screaming projectiles, and the continuous thunder of the guns telling us that something serious was at hand. . . . I started on a run, up a hill, a little swale leading directly to the center. The thunder of the guns was incessant, for the whole air seemed filled with rushing, screaming, and bursting shells. The larger, round shells could be seen plainly as in their nearly completed course they arrived in their fall towards the Taneytown Road, but the long-rifled shells could only be seen in their rapid flight when they "upset" and went tumbling through the air, creating the uncomfortable impression that, no matter whether you were in . . . you were liable to be hit. Every moment or so one would burst, throwing its fragments about in a most disagreeably promiscuous manner or first striking in the earth and rocks.

Meade and his officers got out of the cottage right away, ducking explosions left and right. It was a significant moment in the battle, in a man's life, whether he could recover quickly and move on or simply go into shock, or despair, and fall prey to his emotions. Meade and his officers mounted their horses and simply rode off as fast as they could to open up new headquarters and make more plans for the battle. Meade never flinched. His courage and success impressed all.

Following them was Major St. Clair Mulholland, who later wrote down what he saw.

Major St. Clair Mulholland, Union Army

At this tumultuous moment, we witnessed a deed of heroism as we are apt to attribute only to the knights of the olden time. [I saw] Hancock, mounted and accompanied only by his staff . . . with the Corps flag flying in [his] hands.

Confederate General J. E. B. Stuart was engaged at the rear of the Union line and bottled up, unable to get anywhere, before he and his men finally retreated. There were some successes with the Southern cavalry under Stuart, though, as recounted by Lieutenant. G. W. Beale of the 9th Virginia Cavalry, who was part of General John Chambliss's brigade and riding with Stuart.

Lieutenant G. W. Beale, Confederate Army

We moved forward at a trot, passed Rummel's barn, and engaged the mounted men at close range across a fence. Some of our troops, dismounting, threw down the fence and we entered the field. A short hand to hand [fighting] ensued, but the enemy speedily broke and fled. Whilst pursuing them, I observed another body of the enemy approaching from the right to strike us in the flank and rear. I broke off in company with a portion of our men to meet and check this force.

We soon found ourselves overpowered and fled back, closely pressed on two lines which converged at the barn. I was by General Stuart's side as we approached the barn. My horse fell at this point, placing me in danger of being made a prisoner. At this moment, General [Wade] Hampton dashed up at the head of his brigade. He was holding the colors in his hand, and passed them into the hands of a soldier at his side just as he swept by me. The charge of his brigade, as far as I could judge, was successful in driving the enemy back from that part of the field.

Our brigade reformed on the edge of the woods in which it stood before the charge was made, and this position was held until we were quietly withdrawn at night. Our position commanded an easy view of the barn and the line our skirmishers assumed at the beginning of the battle. We were so near the barn that I rode back to where my horse had fallen to secure, if possible, the effects strapped on my saddle. Later in the evening I sent two of my men to the same spot to search for the body of Pvt. B. B. Ashton, of my company, who was supposed to have been left dead on the field. These facts warrant me in the conviction that we were not driven from the field, as had been contended [later, in news accounts].

Union cavalry were strong everywhere on the field, as observed by General George Custer, riding with the Michigan cavalry. At one point midafternoon, he saw that a huge Confederate cavalry, Stuart's forces, was on a ridge near them and ready to attack.

General George Armstrong Custer, Union Army

To meet this overwhelming force, I had but one available regiment, the First Michigan cavalry, and the fire of Battery M, second regular artillery. I at once ordered the First to charge, but learned at the same moment that similar orders had been given by Brig. General [David] Gregg. As before stated, the First was formed in column of battalions. Upon receiving the order to charge, Colonel [Charles] Town, placing himself at the head of his command, ordered the "trot" and sabers to be drawn. In this manner, this gallant body of men advanced to the attack of a force outnumbering them five to one. In addition to this numerical superiority, the enemy had the advantage of position, and were exultant over the repulse of their cavalry.

All these facts considered, would seem to render success on the part of the First impossible. Not so, however. Arriving within a few yards of the enemy's column, the charge was ordered and with a yell that spread terror before them. The First Michigan cavalry, led by Colonel Town, rode upon the front rank of the enemy, sabering all who came within reach. For a moment, but only a moment, that long heavy column stood its ground. Then, unable to withstand the impetuosity of our attack, it gave way into a disorderly rout, leaving numbers of dead and wounded in our possession, while the First being masters of the field, had the proud satisfaction of seeing the much vaunted "chivalry," led by their favorite commander, seek safety in headlong flight.

I cannot find language to express my high appreciation of the gallantry and daring displayed by the officers and men of the First Michigan cavalry. They advanced to the charge of a vastly superior force with as much order and precision as if going upon parade; and I challenged the annals of warfare to produce a more brilliant or successful charge of cavalry than the one just recounted. . . .

Custer, who graduated last in his class at West Point, was a successful soldier and, surprisingly, became a general at the age of twenty-three. But his biggest fame came at the end of his life, when he died at the Battle of the Little Big Horn, the legendary Custer's Last Stand, in 1876.

Union Lieutenant Alonzo Cushing was badly wounded, his intestines coming out of his stomach. He told his comrade:

Lieutenant Alonzo Cushing, Union Army

Webb, I will give them one more shot.

Cushing fired his cannon, then fell to the ground.

On the Confederate side, Lieutenant Finley reported that the Southerners around him had moved up to the top of Cemetery Ridge, taking and losing ground, determined to split open the Federal line. Somewhere amid the Confederates was General Lewis Armistead, who had just placed his hat on the tip of his sword.

Lieutenant George Finley, Confederate Army

Just as I stepped upon the stone wall, I noticed for the first time a line of troops just joining upon our left. . . . They were from Archer's Tennessee Brigade and a part of Heth's division. This gallant brigade had been terribly cut up in the first day's fight, and there was but a fragment of them left. Some of them, with us, seized and held the stone wall in our front. For several minutes, there were no troops in our immediate front but to our left the Federal line was still unbroken. This fact was impressed upon my mind by my . . . seeing our brave Brigadier General [Richard] Garnett . . . riding to our left, just in my rear, with his eyes fastened upon the unbroken line behind the stone fence and with the evident intention of making such disposition of his men as would dislodge it.

In that instant, suddenly, a terrific fire burst upon us from our front, and, looking around, I saw close to us just on the crest of the ridge, a fresh line of Federals attempting to drive us from the stone fence; but, after exchanging a few rounds with us, they fell back behind the crest, leaving us still in possession of the stone wall. Under the fire, as I immediately learned, General Garnett had fallen dead. Almost simultaneously with these movements, General Armistead, on foot, strode over the stone fence, leaving his brigade most gallantly, with his hat on his sword, and calling upon his men to charge. A few of us followed him until, just as he put his hand upon one of the . . . guns, he was shot down.

Armistead died two days later. Armistead and Union General Hancock, a hundred yards away leading the Union defense [he was shot in the thigh], had long been personal friends. Armistead had asked that if he was killed, his personal effects should be given to Hancock for delivery to his family. Hancock made certain that all of Armistead's belongings were brought to his home and family as soon as possible.

There was hand-to-hand fighting all over Gettysburg on that day. It was particularly vicious on John Rummel's farm. On July 4, surveying his land, he found two dead horsemen, one from the North and one from the South, hands holding each other in death.

John Rummel, farmer

One [was] a Virginian, the other a 3rd Pennsylvania man. They fought on horseback with their sabres until they finally clinched and their horses ran out from under them. Their heads and shoulders were severely cut, and when found, their fingers, although stiffened in death, were so firmly imbedded in each other's flesh that they could not be removed without the aid of force.

Some Confederates did make it to the top of the ridge and broke through the Union line there. As the gray surge made it, the 59th New York, for unexplained reasons, bolted. The New York Independent Artillery Battery, with its five cannon, remained and fired away at the Southerners, killing many. The 71st Pennsylvania had also fled, leaving a large hole in the Union line. They were up against about 3,000 Confederates. The Irishmen of the 69th Pennsylvania rushed into the melee, fighting with rifles, pistols, and bayonets. When their weapons failed, they used their fists in a wild scene of fire and smoke. A regiment of Union Zouaves arrived to help them and many were killed.

Nearby on horseback was Union Lieutenant Frank Haskell, an aide to General Gibbon, who wondered how long the Southerners would be able to maintain the offensive. He was shocked to see men on his own side falling back.

Lieutenant Frank Haskell, Union Army

Were my senses mad? The larger portion of Webb's brigade—my God, it was true—there by the group of trees and the angle of the wall, was breaking from the cover of their works, and without orders or reason, with no hand lifted to check them, was falling back. A fear-stricken flock of confusion. . . . The fate of Gettysburg hung upon a spider's single thread! A great magnificent passion came on me at the instant. . . . My sword, that had always hung idle by my side, a sign of rank only in every battle, I drew bright and gleaming, the symbol of command. . . . All rules and properties were forgotten, all considerations of person, and danger and safety despised; as I met the tide of these rebels. The damned red flags of the rebellion began to thicken and flaunt along the walls they had just deserted . . . I ordered these men to halt and face about and fire, and they heard my voice and gathered my meaning and obeyed my commands. On some unpatriotic backs of those not quick of comprehension, the flat of my sabre fell not lightly. . . . General Webb soon came to my assistance. He was on foot, but he was active. . . . The men that had fallen back, facing the enemy, soon regained confidence in themselves and became steady.

The rush of hundreds of Southerners to that position on top of Cemetery Ridge alerted the Union generals, who sent regiments into the breach and, in a few terrifying minutes, turned back the Southerners. They backed off slowly at first, but then started running down the slope and away from the Federals, never having seized any part of the ridge.

The Southern charge finally lost its steam and the men began to retreat amid heavy cannon and rifle fire from the Federals on top of the ridge.

Lieutenant Finley was aghast at the intensity of the fighting there—and elated at the result.

Lieutenant George Finley

The Rebel column has lost its power. The lines waver. The soldiers of the front rank look round for their supports. They are gone—fleeing over the field, broken, shattered, thrown into confusion by the remorseless fire. . . . The lines have disappeared like a straw in a candle's flame. The ground is fixed with dead, and the wounded are like the withered leaves of autumn. Thousands of rebels throw down their arms and give themselves up as prisoners. How inspiring the moment! How thrilling the hour! It is the high-water mark of the rebellion—a turning point of history and of human destiny.

The Confederates were turned back.

On the battlefield, Pickett seemed thoroughly lost. Major William Poague, an artillery officer, met a dazed Pickett and reported:

Major William Poague, Confederate Army
General: My orders are that as soon as my troops get the hill I am to move as rapidly as possible to their support. But I don't like the looks of things up there.

Pickett stared blankly at the battlefield with an expression of pain.

Major William Poague
What do you think I ought to do under the circumstances?

General George Pickett
I think you had better save your guns.

Pickett nodded at Poague and then rode away and found General Longstreet. Colonel William Youngblood, on Longstreet's staff, was near the two men.

Colonel William Youngblood, Confederate Army
[I heard Pickett say to Longstreet] General, I am ruined. My division is gone—it is destroyed.

Longstreet nodded sadly to him. He understood. It was, after all, something he had expected.

Colonel William Youngblood
There have been few such sights and circumstances as those amid which the two armies found themselves at Gettysburg when the fight was over on Friday afternoon, July 3rd, 1863. . . . Thousands of men were lying unattended, scattered over the field, mingled with broken gun carriages,

exploded caissons, hundreds of dead and dying horses, and other ghastly debris of the battlefield. At once, the poor victims of shot and shell nearest our lines were brought in; others farther out were in due time reached. . . . And the surgeons and nurses . . . kept up their work of ministering and caring for the wounded.

It was possible, as [darkness fell later], to make a bit of a fire here and there in the rear, and boil water for a cup of coffee, which was a boon to be grateful for. While the boys sat or lay on the ground, eating a bit of hardtack and eagerly in their hunger devouring the succulent salt pork, which was about the only nourishment to be secured, relays of men with stretchers, and hundreds of others helping the wounded to walk to the rear, passed back and forth with their bloody freight, now and then a groan or a suppressed shriek telling the story of suffering and heroic fortitude.

Another problem the Confederates had was that, due to the wind, or perhaps the physical placement of hills and gullies, the sound of Union gunfire seemed much louder than it actually was, making the Confederates think, some said, that there were "ten times" as many Union soldiers as there actually were. This feeling caused several Confederate commanders to order their troops back down the hill in defeat.

Lee, his field glasses centered on the crumbling charge, was calm and cool about what appeared to many to be an historic defeat.

Arthur Fremantle, British journalist

Soon afterwards, I joined General Lee, who had, in the meanwhile, come to the front on becoming aware of the disaster. If Longstreet's conduct was admirable, that of General Lee was perfectly sublime. He was engaged in rallying and in encouraging the broken troops, and was riding about a little in front of the wood, quite alone—the whole of his staff being engaged in a similar manner further to the rear. His face, which is always placid and cheerful, did not show signs of the slightest disappointment, care, or annoyance, and he was addressing to every soldier he met a few words of encouragement. . . . He spoke to all the wounded men that passed him . . . I saw many badly wounded men take off their hats and cheer him.

He said to me, "This has been a sad day for us, Colonel—a sad day; but we can't expect always to gain victories."

He was also kind enough to advise me to get into some more sheltered position. Notwithstanding the misfortune which had so suddenly befallen him, General Lee seemed to observe everything, however trivial. When a mounted officer began [beating] his horse for shying at the bursting of a shell, he called out, "Don't whip him, Captain, Don't whip him. I've got such another foolish horse myself, and whipping does no good."

I happened to see a man lying flat on his back in a small ditch and I remarked that I didn't think he seemed dead. This drew General Lee's attention to the man, who commenced groaning dismally. Finding appeals to his patriotism of no avail, General Lee had him ignominiously set on his legs by some neighboring gunners.

I saw General Cadmus Wilcox and an officer who wears a short round jacket and a battered straw hat come up to him and explain, almost crying, the state of his brigade.

What would Lee say? Would he blame the federal artillery ruse? The fact that his men were woefully outnumbered? Fatigue? The turn-back of Stuart's cavalry? Pickett's late arrival? Lee did not. He took on all the blame himself.

Arthur Fremantle, British journalist

General Lee immediately shook hands with him and said cheerfully, "Never mind, never mind, General. All this has been my fault; it is I that have lost this fight. So you must help me out of it in the best way you can."

In this manner, I saw General Lee encourage and reanimate his somewhat dispirited troops, and magnanimously take upon his own shoulders the whole weight of the repulse. It was impossible to look at him or to listen to him without feeling the strongest admiration; and I never saw any man fail him except the man in the ditch.

Even while the last of the Confederate survivors were returning to the lines . . . there was a flurry of action on Lee's extreme right flank as several waves of Union general Judson Kilpatrick's troopers galloped against it.

These ill-advised attacks were smartly stopped. Their only [goal] was to add a good many names to the afternoon's casualty list. Among the fatalities was the newly appointed Union brigadier Elon Farnsworth.

Lieutenant Jesse Bowman Young, Union Army
The battle was now over, but nobody knew it! The repulse of Pickett's charge was the defeat of the Army of Northern Virginia, but . . . the two armies stood at bay, glaring like two wild beasts which had fought one another almost to death, watching for a stroke or a motion and listening for a growl that might indicate further continuance of the struggle. General Meade hardly venture out against the Confederates.

After the defeat of Pickett, General Lee was too weak to undertake any further movement except in retreat, unless he should be attacked.

Union newsman Charles Coffin, who had become friendly with several Union generals, watched the fighting at the top of the ridge and saw the entire charge.

Charles Coffin, *Boston Journal*
Men fire into each other's faces, not five feet apart. There are bayonet thrusts, sabre strokes, pistol shots; cool, deliberate movements on the part of some—hot passionate, desperate efforts with other; hand to hand contests; recklessness of life; tenacity of purpose; fiery determination; oaths, yells, curses, huzzahs, shoutings; men going down on their hands and knees, spinning round like tops, throwing out their arms, gulping up blood, falling—legless, armless, headless. There are ghastly heaps of dead men. Seconds are centuries; minutes, ages . . .

Coffin rode twenty-eight miles on horseback through a rainstorm to catch a train to Baltimore, where he filed his story. It was reportedly the first story that appeared in print about the Battle of Gettysburg.

To the beleaguered Union soldiers on Cemetery Ridge, it was a spectacular success—something they were not accustomed to.

Lieutenant Jesse Bowman Young, Union Army

Cheer after cheer rose from the triumphant boys in blue; echoing from the Round Top, re-echoing from Cemetery Hill, resounding in the vale below, and making the very heavens throb.

General Carl Schurz, Union Army

Here and there, the men began to sing "John Brown's Body."

The song swept weirdly over the bloody field.

General Meade cried "Thank God!" then yelled "Hurrah!" to his troops.

Meade had to be pleased. He had accidentally collided with Lee and his large army and soundly defeated them. He had won what turned out to be the major battle of the war with just three days' experience as head of the Army of the Potomac. He had quickly moved his men into a strong defensive position for Pickett's assault, fooled the Confederates into thinking he had run out of ammunition, survived an explosion at the house he had taken as his headquarters, and turned back the huge Pickett's Charge storming up Cemetery Ridge. He had shown President Lincoln and the other generals that he was a very competent and successful leader of the Army of the Potomac. No one could doubt that.

Confederate General Longstreet was at the bottom of the hill on horseback, watching the carnage through his field glasses.

General James Longstreet

I fully expected to see Meade ride to the front and lead his forces to a . . . countercharge. The Federals were advancing a line of skirmishers which I thought was the advance of their charge. As soon as the line of skirmishers came within reach of our guns, three batteries opened again, and their fire seemed to check at once the threatened advance.

After keeping it up a few minutes, the line of skirmishers disappeared, and my mind was relieved of the apprehension that Meade was going to follow us.

British observer Arthur Fremantle kept his eyes on the field. He wrote that Longstreet maintained a calm and cheerful demeanor during this trying time.

Arthur Fremantle, British journalist

He asked for something to drink. I gave him some rum out of my silver flask, which I begged he would keep in remembrance of the occasion.

Longstreet and many of the men watching the battle knew the day was going very badly for the South.

The dead and wounded were everywhere—on both sides.

Jesse Bowman Young, Union soldier

[R]elays of men with stretchers, and hundreds of others helping the wounded to walk to the rear, passed back and forth with their bloody freight, now and then a groan or a suppressed shriek telling the story of suffering and heroic fortitude.

"Listen boys!" was the shout of one of the men as they lay on the ground. . . . "The fight must be over—listen! There is a band in the rear beginning to tune up. . . ." It was a sight and a situation long to be remembered. The field was covered with the slain; the full moon looked

down with serene, unclouded and softened luster on the field of Gettysburg, trodden down for miles by the two great armies. Surgeons were cutting off limbs, administering whiskey, chloroform, and morphine to deaden pain; hundreds of men were going back and forth from the fields where the actual fighting had occurred, to the rear, with the mangled bodies of the wounded; and about 100,000 men—the survivors—who were left about of 160,000 in the two armies—were waiting to see what would come on the morrow, when suddenly a band of music began to play in the rear of the Union line of battle, down somewhere on Taneytown Road.

Down the valley and up the hill and over the field, into the ears of the wounded and dying men, and beyond our line and into the bivouac of the beaten enemy, the soft gentle and melting tune . . . "Home Sweet, Sweet Home" was breathed from the brazen instruments.

Southern losses were disastrous. There were 7,000 dead and 44,000 wounded that afternoon. As an example, casualties were 941 out of 1,300 in General Garnett's brigade. The 38th North Carolina Infantry retreated to the bottom of the hill with just forty men and a single lieutenant. Company A of the 11th North Carolina, which had entered Pennsylvania with one hundred men, now had only eight, plus one officer. Many companies came back down the ridge with just a single officer alive, or no officers. All told, half the men who engaged in Pickett's Charge were killed or wounded—extraordinarily high numbers.

As thousands of his men came back down Cemetery Ridge, Lee spotted a very tired General Pickett. Lee, like Longstreet, expected the Federals to come after them now that they were beaten. He needed Pickett's help to stop them.

General Lee rode across the open field to Pickett and pointed to a hill.

....

Abraham Lincoln in 1869

General George G. Meade

General James Longstreet

Major General John Fulton Reynolds

General George E. Pickett

General Robert E. Lee

General J. E. B. Stuart

General Joseph Hooker

General John Buford

A map of Gettysburg.

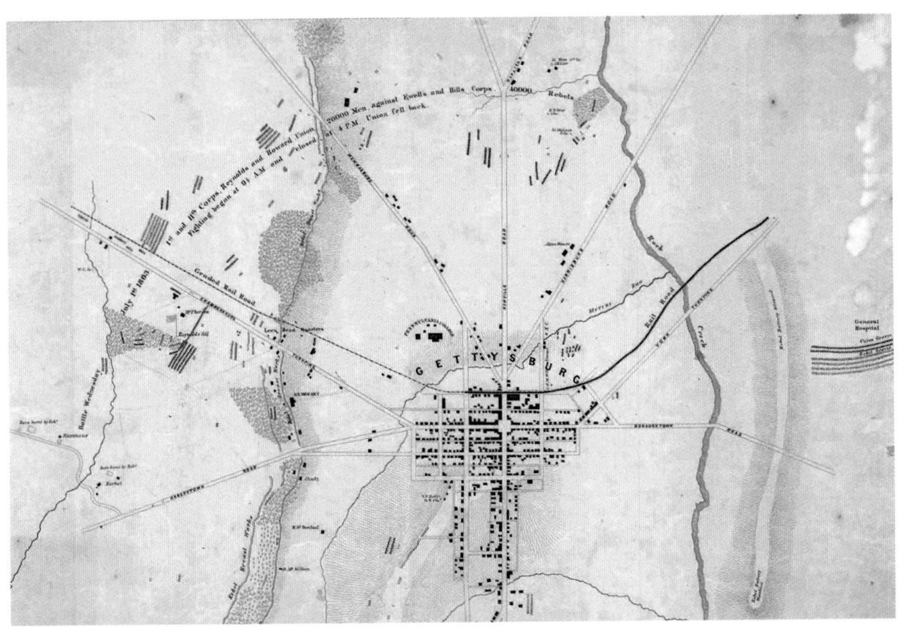

ABOVE AND BELOW: Historic maps of the battlefield of Gettysburg.

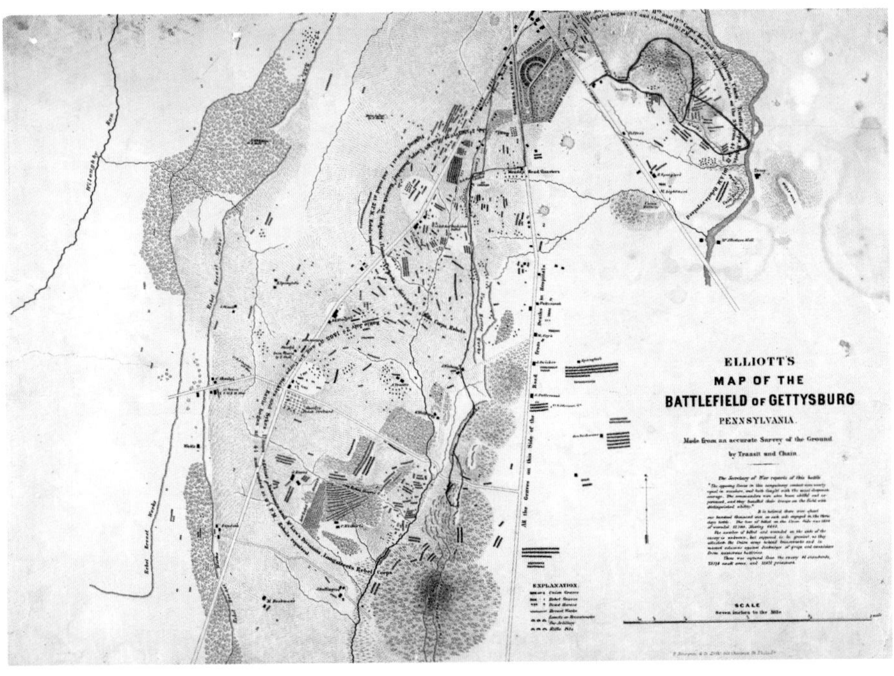

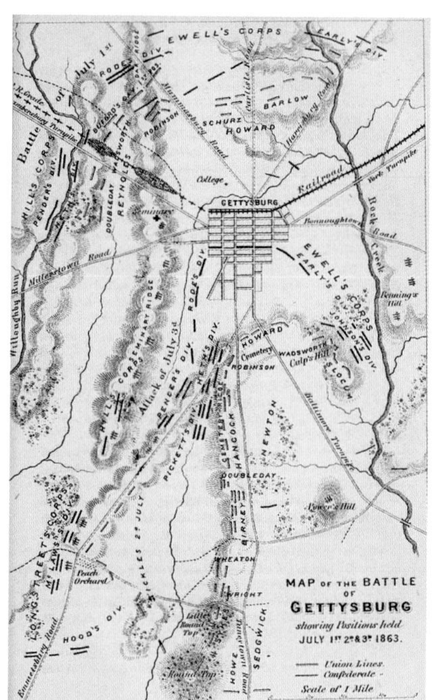

RIGHT AND BELOW: Maps of the Battle of Gettysburg showing positions held by both armies.

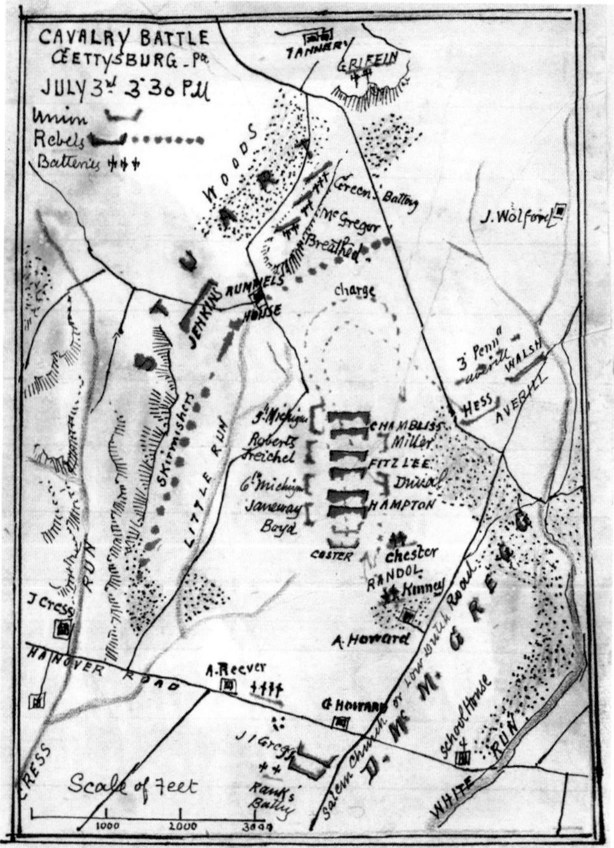

ABOVE: Soldiers preparing cannons on the battlefield.
BELOW: Union artillery unit with horses and cannons.

Cannonballs at Castle Pinckney.

General Pickett taking the order to charge from General Longstreet.

ABOVE: Pickett's Charge.
BELOW: A gun and gunners that repulsed Pickett's Charge at Gettysburg, July 3, 1863.

ABOVE: Brandy Station, Virginia Officers and men of Company K, 1st U.S. Cavalry.
BELOW: General Lee's headquarters.

ABOVE: General Meade's headquarters.
BELOW: President Lincoln visiting Antietam Battlefield.

ABOVE AND BELOW: A photograph and artistic rendering of Lincoln giving the Gettysburg Address.

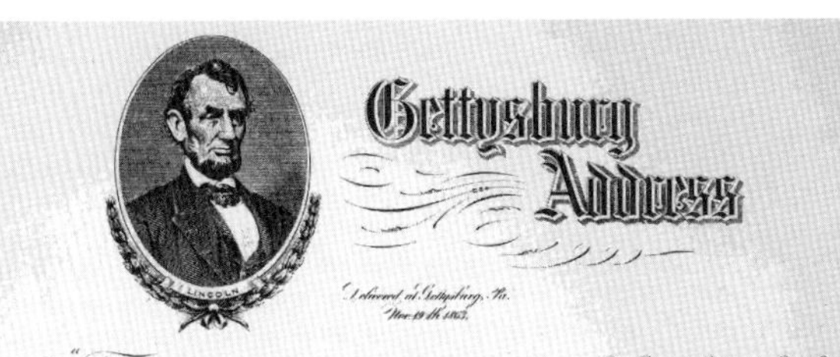

Gettysburg Address

Delivered at Gettysburg, Pa. Nov. 19th 1863.

"Four score and seven years ago our fathers brought forth on this continent a new nation, conceived in liberty and dedicated to the proposition that all men are created equal. Now we are engaged in a great civil war, testing whether that nation, or any nation so conceived and so dedicated, can long endure. We are met on a great battlefield of that war. We have come to dedicate a portion of that field as a final resting place for those who here gave their lives that that nation might live. It is altogether fitting and proper that we should do this. But in a larger sense we can not dedicate, we can not consecrate, we can not hallow this ground. The brave men, living and dead, who struggled here have consecrated it far above our poor power to add or detract. The world will little note, nor long remember what we say here, but it can never forget what they did here. It is for us the living, rather to be dedicated here to the unfinished work which they who fought here have thus far so nobly advanced. It is rather for us to be here dedicated to the great task remaining before us, that from these honored dead we take increased devotion to that cause for which they gave the last full measure of devotion, that we here highly resolve that these dead shall not have died in vain, that this nation, under God, shall have a new birth of freedom, and that government of the people, by the people, for the people, shall not perish from the earth."

ABOVE: The Gettysburg Address.
BELOW: A contemporary marker of the site of Lincoln's address at the dedication of the Gettysburg National Cemetery.

3-inch Ordnance Gun at the Gettysburg National Military Park.

A portion of East Cemetery Hill at Gettysburg National Military Park.

View of East Cemetery Hill at Gettysburg.

A portion of Gettysburg National Cemetery.

The 1869 Soldiers' National Monument at Gettysburg National Cemetery.

Monument to the Confederate forces' Perry's Brigade from Florida at Gettysburg.

The 1893 New York State Monument at Gettysburg.

The Battery K 1st New York Light Artillery monument at Gettysburg.

Monument to the Pennsylvania 73rd Infantry Division (foreground) at Gettysburg.

Monument to Union general Oliver Otis Howard at Gettysburg.

Monument to Union major general Winfield Scott Hancock at Gettysburg.

General Robert E. Lee

General Pickett, place your division in rear of this hill and be ready to repel the advance of the enemy should they follow up their advantage.

Pickett stared blankly at Lee.

General George Pickett

General Lee, I have no division now. . . .

General John Imboden, Confederate Army

We all knew that the day had gone against us, but the full extent of the disaster was only known in high quarters. . . . Our army was not in retreat, and it was surmised in camp that with tomorrow's dawn would come a renewal of the struggle. All felt and appreciated the momentous consequences to the cause of Southern independence of final defeat or victory on that green field. . . .

About 11:00 P.M. a horseman came to summon me to General Lee. I promptly mounted and, accompanied by an aide in my staff, and guided by the courier who brought the message, rode about a mile toward Gettysburg to General Lee's headquarters, On inquiry, I found that he was not there but had gone to the headquarters of General Hill, a mile further south. When we reached the place indicated, a flickering candle visible from the road through the open front of a common wall-tent exposed to view Generals Lee and Hill, seated on camp stools with a map spread upon their knees. Dismounting, I approached on foot. After exchanging ordinary salutations, General Lee directed me to go back to his headquarters and wait for him. I did so, but he did not make his appearance until about 1:00 A.M., when he came riding alone at a slow walk and evidently wrapped in profound thought.

When he [Lee] arrived, there was not even a sentinel on duty at his tent, and no one of his staff awake. As he approached and saw us under a tree, he spoke, reined in his jaded horse, and [moved] to dismount. The effort to do so betrayed so much physical exhaustion that I hurriedly stepped forward to assist him, but before I reached his side, he had succeeded in alighting, and threw his arm across the saddle to rest, and, fixing his eyes upon the ground, leaned in silence and almost motionless upon his equally weary horse. . . . The light from a close by campfire shone full upon his massive features and revealed an expression of sadness that I never had before seen upon his face.

Awed by his appearance, I waited for him to speak until the silence became embarrassing, when, to break it and change the silent current of his thoughts, I ventured to remark, in a sympathetic tone, and in allusion to his great fatigue: "General this has been a hard day on you."

Lee looked up and replied mournfully.

General Robert E. Lee
Yes. It has been a sad, sad day to us.

General John Imboden
He immediately lapsed into his thoughtful mood and attitude.

Being unwilling again to intrude upon his reflections, I said no more. After perhaps a minute or two, he suddenly straightened up to his full height, and, turning to me with more animation and excitement of manner than I had ever seen in him before, for he was a man of wonderful equanimity, he said in a voice tremendous with emotion: "I never saw troops behave more magnificently than Pickett's division did today in that grand charge; and if they had been supported as they were to have been but, for some reason not fully explained to me, were not, we would have held that opposition, and the day would have been ours."

After a moment's pause, Lee added in a loud voice, in a tone almost of agony: "It's too bad. Too bad! Too bad! TOO BAD!"

Then he added, "We must now return to Virginia. As many of our poor wounded as possible must be taken home. I have sent for you because your men and horses are fresh and in good condition to guard and conduct our train back to Virginia."

Lee had sent orders for General Ewell's Corps to withdraw from the town and the Culp's Hill area and meet up with General Longstreet at Seminary Ridge.

◆

Meade's letters on July 3, and subsequent days, noted the huge victory of the Union and large number of prisoners, but he seemed to know that there was still a long war ahead for the Army of the Potomac.

....

General George Meade, in letter

The enemy opened at 1:00 P.M. from about 150 guns, concentrated upon my left center, continuing without intermission for about three hours, at the expiration of which time, he assaulted my left center twice, being, upon both occasions, handsomely repulsed, with severe loss to him, leaving in our hands nearly 3,000 prisoners.

Among the prisoners is Brig. Gen. Armistead and many Colonels and officers of lesser rank.

The enemy left many dead upon the field and a large number of wounded in our hands.

The loss upon our side has been considerable. Maj. Gen. Hancock and Brig. Gen. Gibson were wounded.

After the repelling of the assault, indications leading to the belief that the enemy might be withdrawing, a reconnaissance was pushed forward from the left and the enemy found to be in force. At the present hour, all is quiet. My cavalry has been engaged all day on both flanks of the enemy, harassing and vigorously attacking him with great success.

Notwithstanding, they encountered superior numbers both of cavalry and infantry. The army is in fine spirit.

Union lieutenant L. L. Crounse wrote the day after Pickett's Charge:

Lieutenant L. L. Crounse, Union Army

Another great battle was fought yesterday afternoon, resulting in a magnificent success to the national arms. At 2:00 P.M., Longstreet's whole corps advanced from the rebel center against our center. The enemy's forces were hurled upon our position by columns in mass, and also in lines of battle. Our center was held by General Hancock with the noble, bold Second Army Corps, aided by Col. Doubleday's division of the First Corps.

The rebels first opened a terrific artillery bombardment to demoralize our men and then moved their forces with great impetuosity upon our position. Hancock received the attack with great firmness, and after a furious battle lasting until 5:00 o'clock, the enemy were driven from the field, Longstreet's Corps being almost annihilated. The battle was a most magnificent spectacle. It was fought on an open plain just south of Gettysburg, with not a tree to interrupt the view. The courage of our men was perfectly sublime.

At 5:00 P.M., what was left of the enemy retreated in utter confusion, leaving dozens of flags and Gen. Hancock estimated at least 5,000 killed and wounded on the field. The battle was fought by Gen. Hancock with splendid valor. He won imperishable honor, and Gen. Meade thanked him in the name of the army and the country. He was wounded in the thigh but remained on the field.

The number of prisoners taken is estimated at 3,000, including at least two brigadier generals, Olmsted of Georgia and another—both wounded. The conduct of our veterans was perfectly magnificent. More than 20 battle flags were taken by our troops. Nearly every regiment has one. The 19th Massachusetts captured four. The repulse was so disastrous to the enemy, that Longstreet's Corps is perfectly used up. General Gibbon was wounded in the shoulder. Gen. Webb was wounded and remained on the field. Colonel Hammell, of the 66th New York, was wounded in the arm.

At 7:00 o'clock last evening, Gen. Meade ordered the 3rd Corps, supported by the Sixth, to attack the enemy's right, which was done, and the battle lasted until dark, when a good deal of ground has been gained.

During the day Ewell's Corps kept up a desultory attack upon Slocum on the right, but was repulsed.

Our cavalry is today playing savagely upon the enemy's flank and rear.

Crounse was a soldier, but Samuel Wilkeson was not. He was a journalist. He saw the battle as a horrible defeat for the South, a one-sided victory for the Union.

Wilkeson's nineteen-year-old son, Bayard, was mortally wounded leading his artillery unit on July 1. He later died in a makeshift field hospital that was abandoned by the time his father found his body on July 3. Wilkeson wrote this just three days after his son's death in the battle.

Samuel Wilkeson, ***New York Times***

The experience of all the tried and veteran officers of the Army of the Potomac tells of no such desperate conflict as has been in progress during this day [of Pickett's Charge]; the cannonading of Chancellorsville, Malvern, and Manassas were pastimes compared with this. At the headquarters where I write, sixteen of the horses of Gen. Meade's staff officers were killed by shell. The house was completely riddled. The chief of staff, Gen. Butterfield, was knocked down by a fragment of case-shot. Col. Dickison . . . had the bone of his wrist pierced through by a piece of shell. Lt. Oliver, of Gen. Butterfield's staff, was struck in the head; and Capt. Carpenter, of Gen. Meade's escort, was wounded in the eye.

While I write, the ground about me is covered thick with rebel dead, mingled with our own. Thousands of prisoners have been sent to the rear, and yet the conflict still continues.

The losses on both sides are heavy. Among our wounded officers are Hancock, Gibbon, and a great many others, whose names I feel restrained from publishing without being assured that they are positively on the list of casualties.

It is near sunset. Our troops hold the field with many rebel prisoners in their hands. The enemy has been magnificently repulsed for three days—repulsed on all sides—most magnificently today. Every effort made by him since Wednesday morning to penetrate Meade's lines has failed. The final results of the action, I hope to be able to give you at a later hour this evening.

Lost amid all this was a letter from a Confederate officer that held the defeated General Pickett *in high esteem.*

Confederate officer
[I remember] Pickett's motionless, erect figure under the falling trees and bursting shells. . . .

Wife Sallie told friends that a Union officer told her he could have killed Pickett on the field of battle, but . . .

Union officer
The defeat was complete and total. We can't kill a man as brave as that.

Major John Daniel, Confederate Army
From the height of enjoyment and anticipation, they had suddenly been plunged into the depths of pain and disappointment.

Pickett was angry at everybody for Pickett's Charge and complained about it all in his official report on the disastrous battle. Lee understood his pain.

General Robert E. Lee
No one grieves more than I do at the loss suffered by your noble division in the recent conflict, or honors it more for its bravery and gallantry.

But Lee was also angry with Pickett for the highly critical report and told him to destroy it and a copy, and write a new, less harsh account of the battle.

General Robert E. Lee
We have the enemy to fight and must carefully at this critical moment guard against dissension which the reflections in your report would create.

General Pickett refused to rewrite the report. He wrote in a letter later that month that the Gettysburg campaign was "short but terrible."

General George Pickett
Would that we had never crossed the Potomac. . . . If the charge made by my gallant Virginians on the fatal third day of July had been supported, or even if my other two brigades had been with me, we would have been in Washington and the war ended.

July 4—General Lee's Retreat

Lee could not surrender. The only other option was to retreat out of Pennsylvania, back into his own state of Virginia. Many of his officers were certain that the Union Army would chase them all the way and perhaps defeat them when they reached the Potomac River.

The Army of the Potomac did not follow them.

Lee organized his men the following morning, loaded more than 5,000 of his wounded soldiers onto wagons, and began the withdrawal. The Army of Northern Virginia moved slowly out of Pennsylvania and headed for Virginia. It would never invade the North again; no Southern army would.

Soldiers from both sides walking over the battlefield had strange encounters. Many heard cries of help from men on their side and many others heard cries of help from men on the other side.

Lieutenant Abner Small, Union Army

My duties permitting, I went among the wounded in a small grove on the left of our position, where lay many hurt survivors of the rebel attacking force, men of Pickett's division and of Heth's and Pender's. I proffered what assistance I could. I remember stopping beside one poor fellow who was shot through the body. His wants were few.

"Only a drink of water. I'm cold, so cold. Won't you cover me up?" Then his mind wandered and he murmured something about his mother. Then he had a clear sense of his condition. Would I write to his home and say how much he loved them, and how he died? "Tell them all about it, won't you? Father's name is Robert Jenkins. My name is Will." I thought I heard him say that he belonged to the 7th North Carolina and came from Chatham County.

His words faltered into silence. I covered his face.

In the Confederate ranks there was deep dejection over Pickett's repulse. According to Corporal Napier Bartlett, a cannoneer from Louisiana, many of the men, afraid for their dream of liberty from the Union, were moved to tears. And they were exhausted.

Corporal Napier Bartlett, Confederate Army

The sight of the dying and wounded, who were lying by the thousands between the two lines, and compelled amid their sufferings to witness and be exposed to the cannonade of over 200 guns, and later in the day, the reckless charges, and the subsequent destruction or demoralization of Lee's best corps—the fury, tears or savage irony of the commanders—the patient waiting, which would occasionally break out into sardonic laughter at the ruin of our hopes, seen everywhere around us, and, finally, the decisive moment, when the enemy seemed to be launching his cavalry to sweep the remaining handful of men from the face of the earth: These were all incidents which settled, and will forever remain in the memory. We all remember Gettysburg, although we do not remember and do not care to remember many other of the remaining incidents of the war. . . .

But to return to the battlefield, from which at a little distance, we bivouacked that night. It is true that many of us shed tears in the way in which our dreams of liberty had ended, and then and there gave them a much more careful burial than most of the dead received; yet when we were permitted at length to lie down under the caissons, or in the fence corners, and realized that we had escaped the death that had snatched away so many others, we felt too well satisfied at our good fortune—in spite of the enemy still near us, not to sleep the soundest sleep it is permitted on earth for mortals to enjoy. . . .

Never had the men and horses been so jaded. One of our men who dropped at the foot of a tree in a sort of hollow, went to sleep, and continued sleeping until the water rose to his waist. It was only then that he could be awakened with the greatest difficulty. Battery horses would drop down dead.

So important was our movement that no halt for bivouac, though we marched scarcely two miles an hour, was made during the route from Gettysburg to Williamsport—a march of over 40 miles. The men and officers on horseback would go to sleep without knowing it, and at one time there was a halt occasioned by all of the drivers—or at least those whose business was to attend to it, being asleep in their saddles. In fact, the whole of the army was dozing while marching and moved as if under enchantment or a spell—were asleep and at the same time walking.

President Lincoln's Reaction

In Washington, President Lincoln was happy about the victory but angry because he wanted Meade's army to follow Lee's and smash it—thereby ending the war. But that did not happen.

A week later, in a scathing letter, Lincoln strongly castigated General Meade for letting Lee and his army get away.

President Abraham Lincoln

Again, my dear General, I do not believe you appreciate the magnitude involved in Lee's escape. He was within your easy grasp, and to have closed upon him would, in connection with our other late successes, have ended the war. As it is, the war will be prolonged indefinitely. . . . Your golden opportunity is gone, and I am distressed immeasurably because of it.

To the public, President Lincoln hid his unhappiness with Meade and praised the Northern forces. In a statement he said:

President Abraham Lincoln

. . . such as to cover that army with the highest honor; to promise a great success to the cause of the Union, and to claim the condolence of all for the

many gallant fallen; and for this he especially declares that on this day, He whose will, not ours, should even be done, be everywhere remembered and revered with profoundest gratitude.

Contributor to a US Army veteran's magazine
Had the Army of the Potomac been whipped at Gettysburg, it would have dissolved. Doubtless, some of the volunteer regiments would have held together and made some sort of retreat towards the Susquehanna [River], but the others would simply have deserted en masse in much the same way Napoleon's Army disintegrated after Waterloo. Placing the rebel chieftain . . . at liberty to go where and do what he pleased . . . our army would have been cut in two and in a few days the rebels would have occupied Harrisburg and Philadelphia and terms of peace would have been dictated.

Wild rumors flew everywhere. One had it that Lee was on his way to Washington to occupy it and arrest President Lincoln. Another was that since he was so close to Baltimore in southern Pennsylvania, he would take that city and destroy the north-south railroad lines that ran through it. The strangest and most widely believed rumor was that Lee's army was on its way to Philadelphia and would seize the city.

Telegram to Secretary of War Edwin Stanton
We have information we deem entirely reliable that the rebels are marching on Philadelphia in large force, and also on points on the Philadelphia, Wilmington, and Baltimore railroad. . . . Philadelphia, once taken, they think they will be able to dictate terms [for surrender] to the government.

Over the summer of 1863, Lincoln softened his criticism of General Meade.

President Abraham Lincoln
A few days having passed, I am now profoundly grateful for what was done, without criticism for what was not done. General Meade has my confidence as a brave and skillful officer and a true man.

There was considerable praise for Meade from higher-ups in the army, too, including the commanding general, Henry Halleck.

General Henry Halleck
You [Meade] handled your troops in that battle [Gettysburg] as well, if not better, than any general had handled his army during the war. You brought all your forces into action at the right time and place, which no commander of the Army of the Potomac has done before. You may well be proud of that battle.

General Ulysses S. Grant
I esteem him [Meade] highly and second only to Sherman, and but for his quick temper he would have no superior. And yet with that quick temper goes his quick perception of what is required on the field of battle. . . . He seldom makes mistakes.

There was even praise from the enemy.

Confederate President Jefferson Davis
My idea was that Meade was the most skillful General in the Federal army. General Lee once said to me that he could understand the movements of all the generals in the federal army easier than those of General Meade.

General Robert E. Lee

Meade, in my judgment, had the greatest ability. I feared him more than any man I met upon the field of battle.

On July 4, 1863, both Union and Confederate soldiers tried to bury their dead on the Gettysburg battlefield. It rained—hard. One Union gravedigger turned to another, leaning on his shovel: "This is a terrible, terrible rainstorm in which to bury these soldiers." The second, holding his shovel and looking out over all the dead stacked up on the field, replied, "This is not a rainstorm. It is God crying."

Four months later, Lincoln would visit Gettysburg. He had been asked to make some remarks there as part of a tribute to the troops who lost their lives in and around the town.

PART FIVE
The Gettysburg Address

President Lincoln was not the main attraction on the day he gave the Gettysburg Address. The main attraction, the man everybody came to see and listen to, was the very famous Edward Everett, a statesman and nationally recognized orator from Massachusetts. He was invited to give a speech on the causes of the Civil War. As an afterthought, the committee that invited Everett decided to ask President Lincoln to "deliver a few appropriate remarks" after Everett finished his talk. Lincoln agreed, and decided, as the committee suggested, to keep his speech short and simple and to the point.

The Gettysburg Address was not regarded by Lincoln or anyone else as the most important speech of the Civil War, and certainly not as perhaps the greatest speech ever delivered by an American. No one expected an epic speech on that day, November 19, 1863, just four months after that battle there that claimed the lives of 7,000 men and had tens of thousands of casualties on both sides—about 45,000 men wounded and another 10,000 captured and taken prisoner.

The confrontation turned out to be the bloodiest battle of the entire Civil War. Many who fought in the battle were haunted by its bloodshed and the extraordinary number of casualties. Nineteen-year-old Union soldier Henry Matrau wrote his mother:

Henry Matrau, Union Army

[Gettysburg] was one vast slaughter pen.

Local attorney David Wills headed up a committee to dedicate a national cemetery at Gettysburg, in a ceremony at Soldier's Field, the cemetery's original name. The committee purchased most of the land for the cemetery by the middle of August 1863. (The name was later changed to the Gettysburg National Cemetery, and it is a part of the Gettysburg National Military Park today.) A semicircle was cleared on the field and a platform built to hold all the dignitaries, which included Pennsylvania Governor Andrew Curtin. The governor had visited the battlefield on July 10, less than a week after the battle, and was given a tour. Wills was visibly upset at the condition of the battlefield and the way the dead were rather haphazardly buried. The two men agreed that something had to be done, and done immediately.

Governor Andrew Curtin of Pennsylvania

The feelings were shocked and the heart sickened at the sights that presented themselves at every step. . . . The remaking of our brave soldiers, in the necessary haste in which they were interred, in many instances were but partially covered with earth and, indeed, in some instances were wholly unburied . . . over the fields of arable land for miles around. Humanity shuddered at the sight, and called out for a remedy.

Wills wrote to President Lincoln

David Wills

The several states having soldiers in the Army of the Republic who were killed at the Battle of Gettysburg . . . have procured grounds on a prominent part of the Battle Field for a cemetery.

Our dead are lying on the field unburied. In many instances arms and legs and even heads protrude and my attention has been directed to several places where the hogs were actually rooting out the bodies and devouring them. . . . Humanity calls on us to take measures to remedy this. . . . [We have] the propriety and actual necessity of the purchase of a common burial ground for the dead, now only partially buried over miles of country around Gettysburg. These grounds will be consecrated and set apart to this sacred purpose by appropriate ceremonies on Thursday, the nineteenth instant. . . . It is the desire that, after the oration, you as Chief Executive of the Nation, formally set apart these grounds to their sacred use by a few appropriate remarks.

It appears as though Lincoln knew of the speeches in early September and agreed to deliver one of the talks there.

Governor Curtin, who saw in a Gettysburg memorial cemetery the road to reelection, told Wills to proceed with his plan to develop a cemetery, designed by landscape architect William Saunders, near one that already had existed there for years.

Governor Andrew Curtin of Pennsylvania

[I bestow on you] full power to act upon the suggestions in this letter, and to correspond with the Governors of all the states that had been represented by troops in the battle.

Wills found he had an opponent, and he wanted the speeches to be delivered earlier, at the end of October, but that suggestion was soon scrapped.

The next step was to recruit the famous orator, Edward Everett, to give a talk. Everett was a diplomat, politician, educator, and Unitarian minister from Massachusetts. He said he could not get to Gettysburg on the date of the ceremony, and got Wills to push it back to November 19.

Everett had little regard for President Lincoln as a speaker. He had listened to several Lincoln speeches in the past, and had nothing positive to say.

Edward Everett
These speeches thus have been of the most ordinary kind, destitute of everything, not merely of felicity and grace, but of common pertinence. He is evidently a person of very inferior cast of character, wholly unequal to the crisis.

The opinion was mutual.

President Abraham Lincoln
Now, do you know, I think Edward Everett was very much over-rated. There was one speech in which, addressing a statue of John Adams and a picture of Washington in Faneuil Hall, in Boston, he apostrophized them and said, "Teach us the love of liberty protected by law." [That] was very fine but it was the only good idea. . . .

There was a persistent rumor that Governor Curtin wanted to run against Lincoln in the 1864 election and become president. Many saw his maneuvering for the national cemetery as part of his bold plan to accomplish this. It was the perfect entrée into the race, was it not—tears and sorrow for the slain soldiers.

Lincoln was not "officially" invited to deliver his speech at Gettysburg until a week or so before the scheduled talks, leaving him little time to prepare the speech. But the president still felt he had time enough, and he devoted considerable thought to what he wanted to say to the crowd and to the nation.

Lincoln's decision to travel to Gettysburg was unusual. He delivered few speeches and did not travel far from the White House, for fear of being booed because his Union Army was not winning the war. A proud man, Lincoln did not want to be scorned by the public. He had even turned down an invitation to speak at his hometown of Springfield, Illinois, in front of a friendly crowd because of that fear. The president had many invitations and he turned them all down—except this one.

He accepted the invitation to Gettysburg because he knew the Union victory there was important. It may have changed the course of the entire war.

When Lincoln got off the train at Gettysburg at 6:30 P.M. on November 18, the day before the dedication ceremony, he received a huge reception from a big crowd of people, dressed in all kinds of colorful shirts, jackets, and dresses—mostly Lincoln supporters. The size of the crowd, and its support for the president, surprised many. One woman at the crowded train station wrote:

Susan White, Gettysburg resident
There [were] so many people there that there was no comfort to be taken. There was 20,000 people in town.

Lincoln was taken by carriage to the home of Wills, where he was staying overnight, and was feted at a dinner party for thirty-eight people. While the guests dined, a huge crowd gathered in front of the house to cheer Lincoln and urge him to come out and speak. They were led by students from Pennsylvania College, and made a lot of noise.

They did get the President to leave the Wills house to greet them, but Lincoln had little to say—although he was impressed by the enthusiasm of the crowd for him.

J. Howard Wert, Gettysburg resident
The square on which the Wills house fronted was one dense mass of people eagerly awaiting the appearance of Mr. Lincoln. And when he did appear there was an enthusiastic greeting.

President Abraham Lincoln

I appear before you, fellow citizens, merely to thank you for this compliment. I have no speech to make. In my position, it is somewhat important that I should not say any foolish things [and so I say] nothing at all. I must beg of you to excuse me from addressing you further.

It is unknown where Lincoln wrote all of the address, but it was not on the six-hour train ride on the way from Washington to Pennsylvania—as was long suggested by local lore. He wrote most of the first draft, and several edited drafts, at the White House over the week before the trip to Gettysburg. He might have written some of it over the summer of 1863. In Gettysburg, at the home of Davis Wills, he made last-minute changes and did a final edit of the speech the night before.

During that time, he left the house in darkness and walked to a house where Secretary of State William Seward was staying. Seward had traveled with him from Washington. Lincoln gave Seward the address and he read it. (Seward had done the same thing with Lincoln's first inaugural speech.) No one knows what changes, if any, Seward suggested. Neither man ever referred to that meeting again.

One thing the president wanted to stress in the address, and did, was that death had changed in America. Families were no longer simply burying their dead, but watching, in the war, as the nation buried their dead with them. In fact, he wanted to tell those assembled there the next day that the dead had not just died, but had died together in a cause—the cause of freedom and democracy. His thoughts would forever change the way Americans buried their dead and missed their loved ones.

President Lincoln and his wife, Mary, were no strangers to funerals and cemeteries. They had already buried two of their young sons. Willie, age twelve, had died only a year before. On November 19, Lincoln wore a mourning armband for Willie as he sat very nervously on his horse near the speakers' stand.

In his speech, Lincoln made no mention of the fact that the cemetery was not going to bury the enemy—the Confederates—at Gettysburg. They were buried in a different cemetery and moved to Gettysburg years later.

He also decided not to mention the Emancipation Proclamation, issued that past January, which freed most of the slaves. He knew that all the soldiers fighting in the war, all Americans, saw slavery as one of the main reasons the two armies had clashed throughout the war. He saw no need to bring it up again.

Others still discussed it.

Leigh Webber, Union Army

If all this untold expense of blood and treasure of toil and suffering, of want and sacrifice, of grief and mourning is . . . to result in no greater good than the restoration of the Union as it was . . . [before the war began, that] would result in no real and lasting good.

Amos Hostetter, Union Army

Any country that allows the curse of slavery and amalgamation, as this has done, should be cursed, and I believe in my soul that God allowed this war for the very purpose of clearing out the evil and punishing us as a nation for allowing it.

The next day, the day of the speech, Lincoln and a few others were given a carriage ride around the cemetery and had various sites of the battle pointed out to them. One was Canadian government official William McDougall, who had business in Washington and whom Lincoln invited to join him on his trip to Pennsylvania.

William McDougall

The ground in this vicinity is yet strewn with remains and relics of the fearful struggle—ragged and muddied knapsacks, canteens, cups, haversacks, bayonet sheaths, and here and there fragments of gray and blue jackets . . . hide and skeletons of horses.

Everyone agreed, though, that the president, riding a chestnut horse in the middle of the parade of dignitaries headed to the cemetery, looked bad. He was gawky on any horse. Henry Eyster Jacobs, a student at Gettysburg College, had a close look at the president and shook his head from side to side.

....

Henry Eyster Jacobs

In the long procession . . . as we saw it descending on a hill and then ascending another on Baltimore Street, near the approach to the cemetery, President Lincoln presented a rather comical appearance, with his tall form and long limbs astride a small horse, which had been in some unaccountable way assigned to him. If there had been an accident, he certainly would not have had far to fall.

There was a halt in the parade and, once again, people in the crowd were eager to see and shake hands with the president. Lincoln smiled easily and responded enthusiastically to all, laughing a bit at remarks about how he looked on the horse. Lincoln, who stood six-foot-four, always had problems with his height—even when buying socks to cover his ankles when his too-short pants rode up them when he sat down.

There were dozens of people in the small parade with the president, including Everett, Ward Lamon (Lincoln's bodyguard and personal friend), three cabinet secretaries, Wills, and a handful of congressmen. All thought the twelve-by-twenty-foot speakers' platform was too small to be jammed with all the dignitaries who insisted that they be seated upon it. Some of the students in the parade wound up on it, too.

....

College student

What a piece of luck this was, but, oh, what a jam it was, too. I have never been so wedged in a crowd in my life as I was then. But I was determined to see it through.

It was a nice day with no rain or threat of rain. The sky remained blue all day and the temperature at the time of Lincoln's speech was a crisp 52°F.

Many said they saw Lincoln carrying a large piece of paper with the address written on it. Lincoln often referred to the paper when giving the address. Ward Lamon outlined the usual process President Lincoln followed for each of his speeches—and might have followed for this one at Gettysburg.

Ward Lamon

When Mr. Lincoln had a speech to write, which happened very often, he would put down each thought, as it struck him, on a small strip of paper and, having accumulated a number of these, generally carried them in his hat, or in his pockets, until he had the whole speech composed in this odd way, when he would sit down at his table, connect the fragments, and then write out the whole speech on consecutive sheets.

Edward Everett's speech that day was two hours long—the standard length of a speech in that era. He had given a copy of it to President Lincoln a week or so earlier, thinking, perhaps, that Lincoln would use Everett's speech as a springboard for his own. He did not.

Was Everett's speech that day a good one? Yes, it was.

Henry Eyster Jacobs

The length would have been pardoned and the speech have been commended as being what its author intended, viz, the crowning effort of his life, had President Lincoln not been there.

Was it a long one? Yes it was. Many in the crowd were nearly put to sleep by Everett's two-hour oration. A local resident remarked:

Sarah Jane Hoffman, Gettysburg resident
I thought Edward Everett's speech would never end.

After Everett's talk, it was President Lincoln's turn. When he rose to speak, he received a long and thunderous roar of approval from the crowd. Their positive view of him again surprised the president, who had expected a quiet and somber reception.

Lincoln walked slowly to the speaker's podium, bent a bit because his height towered over all, and looked out at the crowd.

Onlooker
Lincoln stepped slowly to the front of the platform with his hands clasped before him, his natural expression of sadness deepened, his head bent forward, eyes cast to the ground. He held a single large sheet of paper and read without the slightest attempt at declamation.

Abraham Lincoln, the president of the United States, looked out at the massive crowd in front of him and began to deliver, perhaps, the greatest speech in American history.

Henry Eyster Jacobs remembered the appearance of the president well.

Henry Eyster Jacobs
The first few lines of the address were spoken without notes. Then, gradually withdrawing note sheets from his pocket, he held in both hands the sheet on which they were written, making emphatic gestures, not with his hands, which were preoccupied, but by bowing from side to side with his body.

Another onlooker saw him a different way.

Onlooker

He seemed like a prophet of old . . . overmasted by some unseen spirit of a voice from some unseen spirit of the scene. . . . The great assembly listened, most awestruck as to a voice from a divine oracle.

"Four score and seven years ago . . ." Lincoln started.

The crowd was silent and listened, quietly and carefully, to absolutely everything he had to say. They had no idea at that moment what a powerful speech was to come—that the president, in just three minutes, in less than three hundred words, would explain to them what the war, the country, and democracy were all about.

The address stunned the crowd. All were still grieving the battle itself. Finally, someone had not only explained the Civil War to them, but at the same time explained the meaning of freedom, democracy, liberty, and just about everything that held America together.

Coming after Everett's two-hour speech, it was starkly short. And being so short, it had a powerful impact. All the people there in the audience that day never forgot it.

A reporter there tried to copy down everything that Lincoln said in his speech, but had to stop.

Joseph Gilbert, reporter, Associated Press

He had not been known to prepare his speeches in advance and he was expected to speak extemporaneously. . . . I was relied upon to take shorthand notes of his remarks. Fascinated by his intense earnestness and depth of feeling, I unconsciously stopped taking notes and looked up at him.

According to Ward Lamon, many in the crowd did not clap immediately when the speech ended because they were so moved by its power and, at the same time, its sensitivity. The lack of quick applause surprised Lincoln, who was a fine speaker and knew it. He thought the speech tentative, but many on the speakers' platform told him they were "in awe" of it. They all noted the tremendous applause the speech received a moment or two after the initial pause from the crowd.

Many of the nation's leading Northern newspapers printed it in its entirety in their pages the following day, and hundreds more printed it over the next few weeks. Books included it for more than a hundred years, and schoolchildren (I was one of them) had to memorize it and deliver it in front of their classmates.

I asked my eighth grade teacher why we had to do all that. She told us the speech, more than any other document, explained what America was all about. Today, all these years later, I can hear my own voice quivering a bit back then as I came to the end of my recital: ". . . government of the people, by the people, and for the people shall not perish from the earth."

◆

Lincoln was glad that he had been asked to give "appropriate remarks" at Gettysburg. He knew almost nothing about the town besides some sketchy details about the battle, but two years earlier he had given a stirring speech in Philadelphia, where America was born. He saw a talk at Gettysburg as a place to answer questions he had posed in that talk.

President Abraham Lincoln

I would rather be assassinated on this spot than to surrender it.

By "it" he meant Philadelphia—saving it and the kind of government, American democracy, that had been born there. He meant that if a Civil War did come, the Union had to save Philadelphia. He saw Gettysburg, a few hundred miles away, as a place to save Independence Hall, all of Philadelphia, and that government.

British writer William Blackstone defined governments better than most in his writing. He wrote of them:

William Blackstone

The political writers of antiquity will not allow more than three forms of government. The first, when the sovereign power is housed in an aggregate assembly consisting of all the members of a community, which is called a democracy, the second, when it is lodged in a council composed of select members, and then it is styled an aristocracy, the last when it is entrusted in the hands of a single person, and then it takes the name of monarchy. All other species of government, they say, are either corruption of these three.

Lincoln and most Americans believed that the Constitution was the strength of the United States. Guest speaker Edward Everett did, too. He had so said back in 1828.

Edward Everett

Let us then, as we assemble on the birth date of the nation, as we gather on the green turf, once wet with precious blood, let us devote ourselves to the sacred cause, "constitutional liberty." Let us abjure the interests and passions, which divide the great family of American freemen. Let the rage of party spirit sleep today. Let us resolve that our children shall have cause to bless the memory of their fathers, as we have cause to bless ours.

President James Madison

I am not unaware of the circumstances which distinguish the American from other popular governments, as well ancient as modern; and which render extreme circumspection necessary in reasoning from the one case to the other. But after allowing due weight to this consideration, it may still be maintained that there are many points of similitude which render these examples not unworthy of our attention. Many of the defects we have seen . . . are common to a numerous assembly frequently elected by the people, and to the people themselves.

It was that form of government, that "constitutional liberty," Lincoln was referring to in his remarks at Gettysburg.

Lincoln had never agreed that the Southern states needed to secede from the Union. He saw a collection of states made up of men of different views as a strong one. He had he said as much in his speech at Independence Hall in Philadelphia, on his way to being sworn in as president.

President Abraham Lincoln

I shall do nothing inconsistent with the teachings of these holy and most sacred walls. I have never asked anything that does not breathe from those walls. All of my political warfare has been in favor of the teachings that come forth from these sacred walls. May my right hand forget its cunning and my tongue cleave to the roof of my mouth if ever I prove false to those teachings.

The president never forgot that speech and saw the Civil War as the greatest challenge to those American ideals. That's why he went to Gettysburg to deliver his speech—to refocus public opinion on those ideals of the nation.

The president had acknowledged, as Southerners insisted, that it was the right of a nation to break away from itself for some reasons, as the South was doing.

President Abraham Lincoln

This country, along with its institutions, belongs to the people who inhabit it. Whenever they shall grow weary of the existing government, they can exercise their Constitutional right of amending it or their revolutionary right to dismember or overthrow it.

Lincoln hastened to tell all, though, that secession was not a legitimate way to exercise this right of division. Southerners understood Lincoln's ideas, but disagreed.

All the points he made in the speech were built upon ideas he had introduced earlier. Back in 1855, Lincoln had written:

President Abraham Lincoln
On the question of liberty, as a principle, we are not what we have been. When we were the political slaves of King George, and wanted to be free, we called the maxim that "all men are created equal" a self-evident truth; but now, when we have grown fat and have lost all dread of being slaves ourselves, we have become so greedy to be "masters" that we call the same maxim a "self-evident lie." The fourth of July has not quite dwindled away, it is still a great day—for burning fire-crackers!

In his first inaugural address, with secession looming, Lincoln said:

President Abraham Lincoln
Is there any better or equal hope in the world [than our government]? In our present difference, is either party without faith of being in the right? If the Almighty Ruler of Nations, with his eternal truth and justice, be on your side of the North, or yours of the South, that truth and that justice shall surely prevail by the judgment of his great tribunal of the American people.

That, of course, was the basis for the very last line of the Gettysburg Address.

Reading the address again and again, you can see the direct point Lincoln was trying to make; that it was so sad that a war was needed to carry on the ideas of the Declaration of Independence, written so long ago. The nation was still very much divided over the slavery question and other issues, and it was sad that it was costing so much bloodshed, particularly at Gettysburg.

Lincoln's hero was the author of the Declaration of Independence, Thomas Jefferson.

President Abraham Lincoln
[Jefferson was] and perhaps will continue to be, the most distinguished politician in our history . . . The principles of Jefferson are the definitions and axioms of free society. . . . All honor to Jefferson, the man who, in the single people, had the coolness and capacity to introduce into a merely revolutionary document, an abstract truth, applicable to all men and all times. And so to embalm it there, that today and in all coming days, it shall be a rebuke and a stumbling block to the very harbingers of reappearing tyranny and oppression.

Lincoln had frequently asserted that in the Declaration of Independence equality was granted to all as a kind of prelude to actually establishing that equality.

President Abraham Lincoln
They [the fathers] did not mean to assert the obvious untruth, that all men were then actually enjoying that equality, nor yet they were about to confer it, immediately, upon them. In fact, they had no power to confer such a boon. They meant simply to declare the right so that the enforcement might follow as fast as circumstances should permit.

"Four score and seven years ago . . ." he started, hearkening back to the days of the Declaration of Independence and the Revolution, "our fathers brought forth on this continent a new nation, conceived in liberty and dedicated to the proposition that all men are created equal."

Then he left the past for the moment and jumped to the present and why he was here today; why they were all here today.

"Now we are engaged in a great Civil War, testing whether that nation or any nation, so conceived and so dedicated, can long endure."

He had them. His short, eloquent language had won them over. A long silence—no noise anywhere—filled the air.

President Abraham Lincoln

We are met on a great battlefield of that war. We have come to dedicate a portion of that field as a final resting place for those who here gave their lives that that nation might live. It is altogether fitting and proper that we should do this.

But, in a larger sense, we can not dedicate, we can not consecrate, we can not hallow this ground. The brave men, living and dead, who struggled here, have consecrated it, far above our poor power to add or detract. The world will little note, nor long remember what we say here, but it can never forget what they did here. It is for us the living, rather, to be dedicated here to the unfinished work which they who fought here have thus far so nobly advanced. It is rather for us to be here dedicated to the great task remaining before us, that from these honored dead we take increased devotion to that cause for which they gave the last full measure of devotion, that we here highly resolve that these dead shall not have died in vain, that this nation, under God, shall have a new birth of freedom, and that government of the people, by the people, for the people shall not perish from the earth.

The Gettysburg Address has been studied and analyzed for more than one hundred years. Scholar after scholar has interpreted it and reinterpreted it. The purpose of it, in hindsight, was to reunite a Republic embittered by a terrible Civil War and preserve the United States' democratic government.

In 1863, America needed a new birth of freedom and it needed to be reminded that we had something precious in the world—a thriving democracy that was for the people. It had been working since 1789, was working in 1863, would keep working—and still works now.

There is nothing in the Gettysburg Address about the nation's economy, its transition from a farm to an urban society, or anything about slavery. Lincoln assumed that if the Union won the war, all these issues would be resolved. If the Union lost the war, none of them would be resolved. The address was a springboard to a future that, the president believed, was certainly rosier than the Southerners—and many Northerners—believed. All we needed to do, the president reminded everyone that day at Gettysburg, was to stick to the truth of the Declaration of Independence and stick together in this great war. If Americans held together, no one, here or abroad, could defeat us. If American did not stick together, he hinted, the future of America was grim.

And, he said with great power, if government of the people, by the pcople, and for the people held together, in 1863 or in any year, America would remain a splendid democratic institution, the "city on the hill" for all the world to admire.

That, he said, and would say again and again, was a great prize worth fighting a war over. The war was being fought to defend American democracy and to let it shine. In the South, nobody was going to crush democracy, Lincoln assured the world that chilly day in November of 1863.

◆

Lincoln did not mention slavery in his speech, but it was always on his mind. He saw it as a national disgrace.

President Abraham Lincoln

Has anything ever threatened the existence of this Union save and except this very institution of slavery? What is it that we hold most dear amongst us? Our own liberty and prosperity? What has ever threatened our liberty and property save and except this institution of slavery? If this is true, how do you propose to improve the condition of things by enlarging slavery, by spreading it out and making it bigger? You may have a wound or a cancer upon your person and not be able to cut it out lest it bleed to death; but surely it is no way to cure it, to engraft it and to spread it over your whole body.

By the fall of 1863, Lincoln was more convinced than ever that the nation's toleration of slavery had led to the division of its people.

President Abraham Lincoln
If I had had my way, this would never have been commenced. If I had been allowed my way, this war would have ended before this, but we find it still continues and we must believe He permits it for some wise purpose of His own. Mysterious and unknown to us, and though with our limited amount of understanding we may not be able to comprehend it, yet we cannot but believe that He who made the world still governs it.

William Herndon, Lincoln's law partner and biographer
On another occasion, he also wrote that we were all being punished for slavery, that we would not pay for it in money, but in blood.

President Abraham Lincoln
May we not justly fear that the awful calamity of civil war, which now desolates the land, may be but a punishment, inflicted upon us for our presumptuous signs, to the needful end of our national reformation as a whole people?

To another group of people, he said the Civil War was a "terrible visitation on all Americans."

At one point, Lincoln had considered the idea that as the commander in chief of the army and navy he could use his military power to free the slaves. In the fall of 1862 he thought about doing that, right after he chastised one of his commanders for proposing to do the same thing. What prevented him from taking that step? It seems it was his belief that as the civilian president he could not give military orders—and the notion that he was president of all the people, North and South, and could not hurt one side [the South] to benefit the other [the North].

President Abraham Lincoln

If I saw a venomous snake crawling in the road, any man may say I may seize the nearest stick and kill it. But if I found that snake in bed with my children that would be another question. I might hurt the children more than the snake, and it might bite them.

Much more, if I found it in bed with my neighbor's children, and I had bound myself by a solemn oath not to meddle with his children under any circumstances, it would become me to let that particular mode of getting rid of the gentleman alone.

But if there was a bed newly made up to which the children were to be taken, and it was proposed to take a batch of young snakes and put them there with them, I ought to decide.

Yet, Lincoln insisted in the Gettysburg Address that America had been given "a new birth of freedom." With the victory at Gettysburg, it had been "born again."

Lincoln had been talking about a new birth of freedom for years, starting back in 1854 with his talk on the Kansas-Nebraska turmoil.

President Abraham Lincoln

Our Republican robe is spoiled, and trailed in the dust. Let us repurify it. Let us turn and wash it white, in the spirit, if not the blood, of the Revolution. . . .

Let us re-adopt the Declaration of Independence, and with it the practices and policy which harmonizes with it. Let us, North and South—let all Americans, let all lovers of liberty everywhere—join in the great and good work [the "unfinished work" of the Gettysburg Address]. If we do this we shall not only have saved the Union, but we shall have so saved it as to keep and make it forever worthy. We shall have so saved it that the succeeding millions of free, happy people, the world over, shall rise up and call us blessed to the latest generations.

In that same year of 1854, President Lincoln had predicted difficult times between the states of the North and their neighbors to the South.

President Abraham Lincoln
The South, flushed with triumph and tempted to excess; the North betrayed, as they believe, brooding on wrong and burning for revenge. One side will provoke; the other resent. The one will taunt, the other defy; as the aggressor retaliates.

That is exactly what happened in the spring of 1861, at Fort Sumter.

The issues that tore apart the North and South were never far from Lincoln's mind. A short time after the Gettysburg Address, Lincoln wrote a letter to an old friend in Springfield, Illinois, James Conkling, in which he again praised the Union Army's victory at Gettysburg, and at Vicksburg that same week, too, and also applauded the Black troops fighting for the Union.

President Abraham Lincoln
Peace does not appear so distant as it did. I hope it will come soon and come to stay, and so come as to be worth the keeping in all future time. It will then have been proved that among free men there can be no successful appeal from the ballot to the bullet, and that they who take such an appeal are sure to lose their case and pay the cost. And then there will be some black men who can remember that with silent tongue, and clenched teeth, and steady eye, and well-poised bayonet, they have helped mankind on to this great consummation, while I fear there will be some white ones unable to forget that with malignant heart and deceitful speech they strove to hinder it.

◆

Whether they agreed with him or disagreed, Lincoln's aides and secretaries acknowledged his superior skills as a speaker and a writer. John Hay, Lincoln's private secretary, said of the letter the president wrote to Conkling:

John Hay
His letter is a great thing. Some hideously bad rhetoric—some indecorums that are infamous—yet the whole letter takes its solid place in history as a great utterance of a great man.

Lincoln discussed his writings with Hay and another private secretary, John George Nicolay, in late-night trips to their rooms and offices at the White House. Hay, in particular, made many notes in his diary about what Lincoln looked like so late at night. One night the president visited Hay to read him something Lincoln thought was funny, but Hay was just doubled over by the president's appearance in his room well after midnight.

John Hay
[He was] utterly unconscious that he, with his short shirt hanging above his long legs and setting out behind like the tail feathers of an ostrich, was infinitely funnier than anything in the book he was laughing at.

Lincoln was always searching for the right word or words to convey his thinking.

William Herndon, Lincoln's law partner and biographer
He saw all things through a perfect mental lens, There was no diffraction or refraction there. . . . He was not impulsive, fanciful or imaginative, but cold, calm, and precise. He threw his whole mental light around the object

and, after a time, substance and quality stood apart, form and color took their appropriate place, and all was clear and exact in his mind. . . . In the search for words, Mr. Lincoln was always at a loss . . . because there were, in the vast store of words, few that continued the exact coloring, power, and shape of his ideas.

Lincoln's speeches were always easy to listen to and easy to read. He would propose one idea, counter it with a second, counter that one, and go to a third. His most famous statements were all shaped this way. One of the best, perhaps, was from a Senate campaign speech he delivered in 1858.

President Abraham Lincoln

A house divided against itself cannot stand.

I believe this government cannot endure, permanently half slave and half free.

I do not expect the Union to be dissolved—I do not expect the house to fall—but I do expect it will cease to be divided.

It will become all one thing, or all the other.

Either the opponents of slavery will arrest the further spread of it, and place it where the public mind shall rest in the belief that it is in course of ultimate extinction; or its advocates will push it forward till it shall become alike lawful in all the States, old as well as new—North as well as South.

Have we no tendency to the latter condition?

The president followed his own advice in writing the Gettysburg Address. He kept his ideas and his language simple and easy to understand. He made the speech lyrical, something everybody wanted to hear.

◆

The Northern press response to the address was highly emotional and positive. Some disagreed with Lincoln's remark that people would "little note or long remember" what he said that day. Senator Charles Sumner of Massachusetts was one of them.

Senator Charles Sumner of Massachusetts

The world noted at once what he said, and will never cease to remember it. The battle itself was less important than the speech.

One newspaper editor pointed out that it involved a battle won on the nation's birthday.

Editor, *New York Herald*

Our national anniversary, we think, may be celebrated in anticipation today, as in honor of the nation's greatest deliverance.

Many applauded Lincoln not only for his tribute to the troops buried at Gettysburg but his outspoken belief that democracy—American democracy, held sacred since 1776—was not dead. Thousands of men gave their lives to keep it alive at Gettysburg.

Perhaps the local newspaper in Gettysburg, the *Star and Banner*, summed up the Gettysburg Address best.

Editor, *Star and Banner*

The President was most enthusiastically greeted, and when he retired, he did so amid prolonged applause.

Everyone—listeners to it at Gettysburg, congressmen, newspaper editors—remarked that the speech was too short. It was short, the president said, because it did not have to be long.

As Mark Twain once famously pointed out:

Mark Twain
Few sinners are saved after the first twenty minutes of a sermon.

In fact, the Gettysburg Address was so short—just three minutes—for several reasons. First, even Lincoln's two inaugural addresses were not long. He believed in tight speeches that got to the point, quickly and directly. Second, Wills had asked for a short speech and Lincoln gave him one. And third, Lincoln knew he would follow Edward Everett, whose speeches were well-known for being very long.

It was short but poignant, and, to those who read it then, and read it today, very, very powerful—a piece of American history.

Predictably, the Southern newspapers pretty much dismissed the speech. One called Lincoln a buffoon and several accused him of copying a 2,000-year-old speech by ancient Greek politician and general Pericles.

Editor, *Richmond Enquirer*
[It was] the substitution of glittering foil and worthless paste for real brilliance, and the Yankees have an invincible conviction that they are the successors of the Romans in empire and the Athenians in genius.

President Pericles, or rather Abe, made the dedicatory speech, but had to limit his observations within a small compass lest he should tell some funny story over the graves of the immortals.

Editor, *Lynchburg Virginian*
Really, the coarseness of this man would repel and disgust any other people than the Yankees. . . . What a commentary is this on the character of our enemies.

Much later, in 1906, fiction writer Mary Raymond Shipman Andrews published a short story in Scribner's called "The Perfect Tribute," about Lincoln writing and delivering the Gettysburg Address, which gave some historical perspective.

Mary Raymond Shipman Andrews

It will live, that speech. Fifty years from now American school boys will be learning it as part of their education.

It has lived—and has been discussed by hundreds of world leaders. US Secretary of State Dean Rusk said it best.

Secretary of State Dean Rusk

What makes it great and enduring is the simple eloquence with which it restates the idea to which this nation is dedicated: "liberty . . . the proposition that all men are created equal . . . government of the people, by the people, for the people. . . ."

For Southerners, the Battle of Gettysburg loomed large in literature and culture for decades. Perhaps the best piece of Southern writing about it was William Faulkner's novel *Intruder in the Dust.*

William Faulkner

For every Southern boy fourteen years old, not once but whenever he wants it, there is the instant when it's still not yet two o'clock on that July afternoon in 1863, the brigades are in position behind the rail fence, the guns are laid and ready in the woods and the furled flags are already loosened to break out and Pickett himself with his long oiled ringlets and his hat in one hand probably and his sword in the other looking up the hill waiting for Longstreet to give the word and it's all in the balance, it hasn't happened yet, it hasn't even begun yet, it not only hasn't begun yet but there is still time for it not to begin against that position and those circumstances which made more men than Garnett and Kemper and Armistead and Wilcox look grave yet it's going to begin, we all know that, we have come too far with too much at stake and that moment doesn't need even a fourteen-year-old boy to think this time. Maybe this time with all this much to lose and all this much to gain. . . .

◆

On one of my visits to the town of Gettysburg, I drove past a very large stone on the side of the road near the battlefield. I saw some large black painting on it and shook my head, turned to my wife and said, "Look, people even had the nerve to come here to Gettysburg and deface this stone."

We drove closer and closer and slowed down, as did the cars in front of us.

I turned left to see what the graffiti artists had done to the stone. On it, painted in huge black letters for the world to see, were the words:

NONE HERE DIED IN VAIN

Abraham Lincoln's Gettysburg Address

November 19, 1863

Four score and seven years ago our fathers brought forth on this continent a new nation, conceived in liberty, and dedicated to the proposition that all men are created equal.

Now we are engaged in a great civil war, testing whether that nation, or any nation so conceived and so dedicated, can long endure. We are met on a great battlefield of that war. We have come to dedicate a portion of that field as a final resting place for those who here gave their lives that that nation might live. It is altogether fitting and proper that we should do this.

But, in a larger sense, we can not dedicate, we can not consecrate, we can not hallow this ground. The brave men, living and dead, who struggled here, have consecrated it, far above our poor power to add or detract. The world will little note, nor long remember what we say here, but it can never forget what they did here.

It is for us the living, rather, to be dedicated here to the unfinished work which they who fought here have thus far so nobly advanced. It is rather for us to be here dedicated to the great task remaining before us, that from these honored dead we take increased devotion to that cause for which they gave the last full measure of devotion, that we here highly resolve that these dead shall not have died in vain, that this nation, under God, shall have a new birth of freedom, and that government of the people, by the people, for the people shall not perish from the earth.

Bibliography

Basler, Roy, ed. *The Collected Works of Abraham Lincoln*. 8 vols. New Brunswick, NJ: Rutgers University Press, 1953.

Beale, Howard K., and Alan Brownsword, *The Diary of Gideon Welles*. New York: W. W. Norton, 1960.

Beale, Howard, ed. *The Diary of Edward Bates, 1859–1866*. Annual Report of the American Historical Association for the Year 1930. Vol. IV. Scotts Valley, Calif.: CreateSpace Independent Publishing Platform, 2013.

Bernard, George. *The Gettysburg Campaign*. Pittsburgh Enterprise, 1894.

Blackford, W. W. *War Years with JEB Stuart*. New York: Charles Scribner's Sons, 1945.

Boatner, Mark. *The Civil War Dictionary*. New York: Vintage, 1959.

Boritt, Gabor. *The Gettysburg Gospel: The Lincoln Speech that Nobody Knows*. New York: Simon & Schuster, 2006.

Bowden, Scott, and Bill Ward. *Last Chance for Victory: Robert E, Lee and the Gettysburg Campaign*. Cambridge, Mass.: Da Capo Press, 2001.

Broadhead, Sarah. *The Diary of a Lady from Gettysburg, Pennsylvania from June 15 to July 15, 1863*. Farmington, Mich.: Sabin Americana, 2012.

Brown, Kent. *Meade at Gettysburg: A Study in Command*. Chapel Hill: University of North Carolina Press, 2022.

Catton, Bruce. *Gettysburg: The Final Fury*. Garden City, NY: Vintage, 2013.

Chamberlain, Joshua. *Through Blood & Fire*. Mechanicsburg, Penn.: Stackpole, 1996.

Chamberlain, Joshua. *The Passing of the Armies. An Account of the Final Campaign of the Army of the Potomac*. New York: Bantam, 1993.

Clark, Champ. *Gettysburg: The Confederate High Tide*. Alexandria, Va.: Time-Life Books, 1985.

Coffin, Howard. *Nine Months to Gettysburg: Stannard's Vermonters and the Repulse of Pickett's Charge*. Woodstock, Vt.: Countryman Press, 1997.

Commager, Henry Steel, ed. *The Blue and the Gray: The Story of the Civil War as Told by Participants*. New York: Fairfax Press, 1982.

Conant, Sean, ed. *The Gettysburg Address*. New York: Oxford University Press, 2015.

Connelly, Thomas. *The Marble Man: Robert E. Lee and His Image in American Society*. Baton Rouge: Louisiana State University Press, 1978.

Cox, John D. *Culp's Hill: The Attack and Defense of the Union Flank, July 2, 1863*. Cambridge, Mass.: Da Capo, 2003.

Dana, Charles. *Recollections of the Civil War, with Leaders in Washington and in the Field in the Sixties*. Lincoln: University of Nebraska Press, 1960.

Davis, Burke. *Jeb Stuart: The Last Cavalier*. Ithaca, NY: Burford Books, 2020.

Doubleday, Abner. *Gettysburg Made Plain*. New York: Century Company, 1909.

Douglas, Henry. *I Rode with Stonewall*. Chapel Hill: University of North Carolina Press, 1940.

Dowdey, Clifford, and Louis Manarin, eds. *The Wartime Papers of Robert E. Lee*. Cambridge, Mass.: Da Capo, 1961.

Dowdey, Clifford. *Lee: A Biography*. New York: Bonanza Books, 1985.

Dowdey, Clifford. *Death of a Nation: The Story of Lee and His Men at Gettysburg*. Baltimore: Butternut and Blue, 1988.

Downey, Fairfax. *The Guns at Gettysburg*. New York: Collier, 1962.

Dudley, William. *The Iron Brigade at Gettysburg, and Official Report of the Part Borne by the First Brigade 1st Division, 1st Army Corps, Army of the Potomac in Action at Gettysburg, Pennsylvania, July 1, July 2 and July 3, 1863*, 1879 reprint. Baltimore: Butternut and Blue, 2001.

Dyer, Frederick. *Compendium of the War of the Rebellion*. New York: Thomas Yoseloff, 1959.

Early, Jubal. *Autobiographical Sketch and Narrative of the War Between the States*. Philadelphia: J.B. Lippincott, 1912.

Eaton, Clement. *Jefferson Davis*. New York, Free Press, 1977.

Eggleston, George. *A Rebel's Recollections*. New York: G.P. Putnam, 1878.

Ewell, Richard. *Letters of General Richard Ewell*. Knoxville: University of Tennessee Press, 2012.

Feibeger, Gustav. *The Campaign and Battle of Gettysburg*. New Oxford, Penn.: Bloodstone Press, 1984.

Fitzhugh, Lee. *General Lee*. Greenwich, Conn.: Fawcett, 1964.

Fleming, George. *The Life and Letters of Alexander Hays*. Pittsburgh: Gilbert Adam Hays, 1919.

Foote, Shelby. *The Civil War, A Narrative: Red River to Appomattox*. New York: Random House, 1974.

Fox, William D. *New York at Gettysburg*, Albany: FB & C Ltd., 1902.

Freeman, Douglas Southall. *Lee's Lieutenants*. 3 vols. New York: Scribner, 1972.

Fremantle, James. *Three Months in the Southern States, April-June, 1863*. Lincoln: University of Nebraska Press, 1991.

Gallagher, Gary. *Lee and His Army in Confederate History*. Chapel Hill: University of North Carolina Press, 2001.

Gallagher, Gary, ed. *The Third Day at Gettysburg & Beyond*. Chapel Hill: University of North Carolina Press, 1994.

Gibbon, John. *Personal Recollections of the Civil War*. New York: G.P. Putnam, 1928.

Giles, Val. *Rags and Hope: The Recollections of Val C. Giles: Four Years with Hood's Brigade, Fourth Texas Infantry, 1861–1864*. New York: Cowan-McCann, 1961.

Glazier, Willard. *Three Years in the Federal Cavalry*. New York: R.H. Ferguson, 1870.

Gordon, John. *Reminiscences of the Civil War*. New York: Charles Scribner, 1903.

Gordon, Lesley. *General George E. Pickett in Life and Legend*. Chapel Hill: University of North Carolina Press, 1998.

Gorhan, George. *Life and Public Services of Edwin M. Stanton*. Boston: Houghton Mifflin, 1899.

Gragg, Rod. *Covered with Glory: The 26th North Carolina Infantry at the Battle of Gettysburg*. New York: HarperCollins, 2000.

Gragg, Rod. *The Illustrated Gettysburg Reader: An Eyewitness History of the Civil War's Greatest Battle*. Washington: Regnery History, 2013.

Hancock, Almira. *Reminiscences of Winfield Scott Hancock by His Wife*. New York: Charles Webster, 1887.

Haskell, Frank. *The Battle of Gettysburg*. Bruce Catton, ed. Boston: Houghton Mifflin, 1958.

Haskell, John C. *The Haskell Memoirs*. New York: Putnam, 1960.

Hassler, William. *A. P. Hill: Lee's Forgotten General*. Chapel Hill: University of North Carolina Press, 1957.

Hebert, Walter. *Fighting Joe Hooker*. Indianapolis: Bobbs-Merrill, 1944.

Hess, Earl. *Pickett's Charge—The Last Attack at Gettysburg*. Chapel Hill: University of North Carolina Press, 2001.

Hoke, Jacob. *The Great Invasion of 1863*. Dayton, Ohio: W.J. Shuey, 1887.

Hood, John Bell. *Advance and Retreat: Personal Experiences in the United States and Confederate States Armies*. New Orleans: G.T. Beauregard, 1880.

Inman, Arthur, ed. *Soldier of the South: General Pickett's War Letters to His Wife*. New York: Houghton Mifflin, 1928.

Johnson, Robert, and Clarence Buell. *Battles and Leaders of the Civil War*, Vol. 3. New York: Castle Books, 1956.

Jones, J. B. *A Rebel War Clerk's Diary*. New York: J.P. Lippincott, 1866.

Kantor, MacKinlay. *Gettysburg*. New York: Random House, 1952.

Kegel, James. *North with Lee and Jackson: The Lost Story of Gettysburg*. Mechanicsburg, Penn.: Stackpole Books, 1996.

Knorowski, Carolyn, ed. *Gettysburg People*. New York: Rowman & Littlefield, 2015.

Lee, Robert E. *Recollections and Letters of General Robert E. Lee*. New York: Doubleday, Page & Co., 1904.

Long, Armistead. *Memoirs of Robert E. Lee*. New York: J.M. Stoddard, 1886.

Long, E. B. *The Civil War, Day by Day, An Almanac, 1861–1865.* Garden City, NY: Doubleday, 1971.

Longacre, Edward. *General John Buford, a Military Biography.* Conshohocken, Penn.: Combined Books, 1995.

Longacre, Edward. *The Man Behind the Guns: A Military Biography of General Henry Hunt, Chief of Artillery, Army of the Potomac.* Cambridge, Mass.: Da Capo Press, 2003.

Longacre, Edward. *Joshua Chamberlain: The Soldier and the Man.* Cambridge, Mass.: Da Capo Press, 2003.

Longstreet, James. *From Manassas to Appomattox: Memoirs of the Civil War in America.* Philadelphia: J.P. Lippincott, 1896.

McClellan, H. B. *General J. E. B. Stuart at Gettysburg.* New York: CreateSpace, 2015.

Meade, George. *The Life and Letters of George Gordon Meade.* New York: Charles Scribner's Sons, 1913.

Most Fearful Ordeal: Original Coverage of the Civil War by Writers and Reporters of The New York Times, The. New York: St. Martin's Press, 2004.

Murphy, Jim. *The Long Road to Gettysburg.* New York: Clarion Books, 1992.

Nesbitt, Mark. *35 Days to Gettysburg: The Campaign Diaries of Two American Enemies.* Mechanicsburg, Penn.: Stackpole Books, 1992.

Pfanz, Don. *Richard Ewell: A Soldier's Life.* Chapel Hill: University of North Carolina Press, 1998.

Pfarr, Cory. *Longstreet at Gettysburg: A Critical Reassessment.* Jefferson City, NC: MacFarland and Company, 2019.

Pfisterer, Frederick, ed. *New York in the War of the Rebellion, 1861–1865.* Albany, NY: Weed, Parsons & Co., 1890.

Pickett, George, and LaSalle Corbell Pickett. *The Heart of a Soldier, as Revealed in the Intimate Letters of George E. Pickett.* New York: Seth Moyle, 1913.

Pierce, Terry. *Without Warning: Saga of Gettysburg, A Reluctant Union Hero, and the Men He Inspired.* Stanwood, Wash.: Heart Ally Books, 2020.

Piston, William. *Lee's Tarnished Lieutenant: James Longstreet and His Place in Southern History.* Athens: University of Georgia Press, 1987.

Raus, Edmund Jr. *A Generation on the March: The Union Army at Gettysburg.* Gettysburg, Penn.: Thomas Publications, 1996.

Reardon, Carol. *Pickett's Charge in History and Memory.* Chapel Hill: University of North Carolina Press, 1997.

Samito, Christian, ed. *Fear Was Not in Him: The Civil War Letters of Francis Barlow.* New York: Fordham University Press, 2006.

Scott, James. *The Story of the Battles at Gettysburg.* Harrisburg, Penn.: Telegraph Press, 1927.

Sears, Stephen W. *Gettysburg.* New York: Houghton Mifflin, 2003.

Skelly, Daniel. *A Boy's Experiences During the Battle of Gettysburg.* Gettysburg, Penn.: Skelly, 1932.

Sorrel, Moxley. *Recollections of a Confederate Staff Officer.* New York: Neale Publishing, 1905.

Taylor, Walter. *Four Years with General Lee.* New York: D. Appleton & Co., 1878.

Trudeau, Noah. *Gettysburg: A Testing of Courage.* New York: HarperCollins, 2002.

Wert, Jeffrey. *Cavalryman of the Lost Cause: A Biography of J. E. B. Stuart.* New York: Simon and Schuster, 2008.

Wheeler, Richard. *Witness to Gettysburg.* New York: Harper & Row, 1987.

Wiley, Bell Irvin. *The Life of Billy Yank: The Common Soldier in the Union Army.* Baton Rouge: Louisiana State University Press, 1978.

Wiley, Bell Irvin. *The Life of Johnny Reb: The Common Soldier of the Confederacy.* Baton Rouge: Louisiana State University Press, 1978.

Index

D

E

F